A Primer of Sociometry

A Primer
of Sociometry

Second Edition

Mary L. Northway

University of Toronto Press

Preface

SOCIOMETRY is one of the most fascinating techniques for the study of social relationships. Because of its interest and deceptive simplicity, teachers, group workers, and indeed research students often blithely decide to use it and later are stunned by the meticulous care it requires and by the apparently complex statistics it involves.

During the last twenty years a wealth of sociometric literature has accumulated. The very abundance of information may add to the novice's confusion as he finds himself enmeshed in reading controversies about technical problems which blind him to the fundamental philosophy and principles of procedure. Also, during these twenty years sociometry and its offspring, sociodrama and psychodrama, and related applied techniques have been found so useful in both educational and therapeutic situations that the novice imagines sociometry to be a magic potion by which all social ills can be cured; often in his genuine concern for human welfare he hastens to administer it at once before understanding the ingredients for a correct prescription.

Too, authorities in this area believe that the sociometric approach will revolutionize our understanding of the nature of human society; they also suggest that the lives of individuals and groups are to be rearranged on the basis of its discoveries. If sociometry is to be so powerful an influence it is essential that its techniques have the acuity of precision tools and that its discoveries be the outcome of genuine and accurate scientific data. No technique is validated merely by the amount of enthusiasm it engenders; such enthusiasm, however, is important in so far as it creates the patience, toil, and honesty which are required for truth to be approximated.

We have purposely called this booklet a primer. It is a *prim-er* in that it introduces the student to the basic principles and practices of sociometry and guides him gently into the intricacies of literature in this field. We have included little that is new; rather we hope that we have made what is already available more accessible. The booklet, it is hoped, will serve also as a *pri-mer* to set the readers' mental mechanisms in action so that the problems which at present are intriguing and baffling will be resolved and increased clarity in our understanding of human relationships be achieved.

All writers in this field are influenced by the challenging inspiration of Moreno and his associates; we, however, are also particularly indebted to our own colleagues and students, past and present. The

references we have quoted form our expression of individual acknowl-
edgement. For arranging for funds from the federal Mental Health
grants to be used to finance part of the cost of publishing this booklet,
and for providing opportunity and incentive for compiling it, the writer
is grateful to Dr. W. E. Blatz and the staff of the Institute of Child
Study. We are deeply indebted to Mrs. Helen Bott who in her pioneer-
ing studies at the Institute of children's social development set a high
standard for all subsequent research in this area and who was
responsible for introducing us to the field of sociometry.

M. L. N.

Institute of Child Study
University of Toronto
Toronto, Canada
May, 1952

Preface to the second edition

THIS BOOK was first published fifteen years ago; it has been reprinted twice and translated into Italian and French. It was the first of the "how to do it" books in sociometry and has been succeeded by much more extensive volumes by Dr. Evans (*Sociometry in Education*) in the United Kingdom, Professor Gronlund (*Sociometry in the Classroom*) in the United States, as well as by our own later small manual *Sociometric Testing: A Guide for Teachers* in Canada.

Great progress has been made in sociometry and in social sciences related to it during the last fifteen years. To undertake a complete revision that would bring the Primer up to date, would necessitate writing a large new book. In this revision, I have taken into consideration some of the more recent developments relevant to the matters discussed in the original manuscript. I have not attempted to describe these fully, or perhaps even adequately, but rather have tried to indicate to the reader the sources he can consult in order to become familiar with them. I have also made any necessary corrections that came to light as a result of later studies; deleted references that are no longer accessible or which have been themselves up-dated, and added references to more recent material.

A review of the growth of sociometry up to the late 1950's is given by Jiri Nehnevajsa in the *Sociometry Reader*. Nehnevajsa's concluding statement indicates the extent and importance of this growth: "Sociometry has thus been not only a field of study in its own right. Not only has it directly enriched our modern research methodology and pushed some of the barriers of the unknown. It has, at the same time, been the fertile soil for many related activities—it has permeated all of contemporary behavioral research to some extent. In its youth of thirty some years, sociometry has done more than well, indeed. Yet its growth has just begun."

For more recent developments, especially those in the United States, the journal *Sociometry* should be consulted, particularly for the years after 1960.

Sociometry is used in many part of the world, including Germany, Norway, Japan, the Phillipines, and Thailand. It has been applied to many types of social groupings: industry, the services, communities, parishes, mental hospitals and college residences. This is not surprising, for all human beings live in some form of social organization and, as sociometry is a "culture free" instrument which can adapt its criteria for association to situations that really exist in any social structure, it has universal appropriateness. That our own local efforts have been concerned with the sociometry of childhood is simply an outcome of our own fancy and the opportunities available to us.

From the viewpoint of my own biases, my perceptions of the advances made in sociometry through recent years are as follows. First, the progress that has been made in sophisticated research design and mathematics should be noted. Moreno always spoke of the social atom; the complexity of sociometric interrelations may indeed be likened to those of the chemical molecule, and mathematics is enabling them to be handled in this fashion. The spearhead of this development is in the United States. The advances being made along these lines are yielding basic and revealing information regarding the laws and properties of social interrelations and interaction. Their very sophistication and foreign linguistics have perhaps unjustly made them a threat to the person whose main concern is to use sociometric techniques to gain insight into understanding groups with whom he is practically concerned. This flight into obscurity is typical of this stage in the growth of the behavioural sciences. As Barbara Tuchman says, "Let us beware of the plight of our colleagues, the behavioural scientists, who by use of a proliferating jargon have painted themselves into a corner—or isolation ward—of unintelligibility. They know what they mean but no one else does. . . . No matter how illuminating their discoveries, if the behavioral scientists write only to be understood by one another, they must come to the end of the Mandarins."* My own formulation of this attitude appeared in a recent book, "The form of the scientific article is as constricting as that of a sonnet, and its content rarely as interesting."†

Yet I do not believe this remoteness should be a threat. Science must advance and it must first do so using its own language. The task which remains is to translate accurately from this and communicate its discoveries to the practitioners. This has always been a pattern of sociometrists since Moreno developed his sociodrama and group psychotherapy and Helen Jennings her guide for fostering mental health in schools.

The second line of sociometric advance makes a vivid contrast: this is the application of sociometry to education. I viewed this most clearly in Great Britain where sociometry is being directed to use through the Institutes of Education, in the schoolroom and in school yards. A whole generation of teachers is being trained to perceive a class as a social

*Saturday Review, February 25, 1967.
†Laughter in the Front Hall, Longmans of Canada, 1966.

group with its myriad opportunities for guidance of the learning of social relationships and growth in social appreciation.

My viewpoint on advances in sociometry cannot fail to be influenced by my near as well as my far vision. Through the last decade at Toronto we have concentrated on long term studies of children's sociometric relations and the changes in these over periods of as much as ten years. Thus we have added a *time dimension* which the use of the electronic computer has enabled us to investigate more fully. Such findings as we have made are now being prepared for publication. Another interest which is novel, and I am aware of its being followed only in our local setting, is the use of the individual sociogram, along with such familiar devices as intelligence and personality tests, rating scales and interviews as a tool for guidance counselling. My colleagues who employ it in this way assure me that it is an extremely useful device for this purpose; I look forward to learning in detail about the value they have found in it.

One cannot predict any revision that might be needed in this primer in, let us say, 1980. Increased scientific knowledge there will certainly be; greater mathematical progress will have been made, more use have been made of sociometry in human settings. We may be able to demonstrate its value as an instrument for use in areas of social conflict—in organizations, between management and labour, in racial and international disputes. Yet the main sociometric revelation which will be described in 1980 has already been made. Sociometry reveals dramatically and factually that human individuals live and move and have their fullest being only in their associations with one another. "No man is an Iland." Can we make this social reality the basis of our living philosophy? If we can, there is hope for man's future; if not, there might well be no 1980.

M.L.N.

Institute of Child Study
University of Toronto
June, 1967

The editorial and clerical work on this revision have been supported in part by Grants 71 and 103 from the Ontario Mental Health Foundation.

Contents

PREFACE / v

PREFACE TO THE SECOND EDITION / vii

1 What is a sociometric test? / 3

2 How to design a sociometric test / 5

3 How to administer the test / 9

4 How to organize the results / 12

5 What to do with the scores / 15

6 The reliability and validity of a sociometric test / 21

7 The target sociogram / 26

8 How to interpret the results / 33

9 What does sociometry measure? / 45

10 The contribution of sociometry / 50

APPENDICES

A Suggested problems for research / 55

B Suggestions for reporting a sociometric study / 57

C Additional notes / 58

A Primer of Sociometry

1
What is a sociometric test?

A SOCIOMETRIC TEST is a means for determining the degree to which individuals are accepted in a group,* for discovering the relationships which exist among these individuals, and for disclosing the structure of the group itself. As well as being highly accurate, it has the added values of simplicity in use and speed in administration. It has been used with school classroom groups; at summer camps; in industries; in the military services; in villages and communities; with committees; and in nursery schools. It is most satisfactory for groups with defined boundaries, in which the individuals know each other at least by name and continue with some cohesion over a reasonable period of time; it is less satisfactory for very large groups and for ill-defined groups, such as audiences; and not at all satisfactory for groups which meet only on one or two occasions.

Sociometry was established by J. L. Moreno in *Who Shall Survive?*, 1934. This book was the culmination of a long period of preparation during which the sociometric approach had been used by Moreno himself and by others in the field of social psychology and sociology. Since 1934, sociometry has rapidly expanded in its scope and been refined in its techniques. This development is reflected in the wealth of literature, and can be traced through the fifteen volumes of the *Journal of Sociometry*, the monographs issued by the Sociometric Institute, and through the articles which appear sporadically but with increasing frequency in other journals. A bibliography of some one hundred and sixty significant articles is given by Helen Hall Jennings in the second edition of her book *Leadership and Isolation*.

The sociometric technique consists in asking each individual in a group to state with whom among the members of the group he prefers to associate for specific activities or in particular situations. From the answers obtained, the choices each individual receives are added to give him a sociometric score, and the choices made between or among particular individuals are recorded. These results are often depicted on a "sociogram."

*This is called their *sociometric status*.

Basic Library of Sociometry

EVANS, K. M. *Sociometry in Education.* London: Routledge & Kegan Paul, 1962.

GRONLUND, N. E. *Sociometry in the Classroom.* New York: Harper, 1959.

JENNINGS, HELEN H. *Leadership and Isolation: A Study of Personality in Interpersonal Relations.* New York: Longmans, Green, 1943. Second edition 1950.

LINDZEY, G. and BORGATTA, E. F. "Sociometric Measurement." Chapter XI in G. LINDZEY, *Handbook of Social Psychology.* Cambridge, Mass.: Addison-Wesley, 1954.

MORENO, J. L. *Who Shall Survive? A New Approach to the Problem of Human Relationships.* Beacon, New York: Beacon House, 1934. A revised and greatly enlarged edition was published in 1953 with the subtitle *Foundations of Sociometry, Group Psychotherapy and Sociodrama.* This includes over 700 references to literature in the sociometric area.

—— ed. *The Sociometry Reader.* Glencoe: Free Press, 1960, pp. 773. A collection of the most important articles in the field of sociometry. The selections range from the foundations of the discipline, through methodology and the major areas of exploration, to its historical development.

NORTHWAY, M. L. and WELD, L. *Sociometric Testing: A Guide for Teachers.* Toronto: University of Toronto Press, 1957.

Sociometry—A Journal of Inter-Personal Relations, Vol. I–XV. New York: Beacon House; Vols. I–XVIII, 1937–55. In 1955 this journal was transferred to the American Sociological Association and given the subtitle, *A Journal of Research in Social Psychology.* Vols. XIX–XXX, 1955–67.

2

How to design a sociometric test

FROM ACTUAL KNOWLEDGE of a group, select three or four areas in which the members have or could have real opportunity for associating. These areas must be pertinent to the exact group. Thus for most school children "playing together at recess" would probably be suitable, but for workers in a certain industry "working at the same bench" would be more appropriate. The areas selected should include different aspects of possible association such as work, play, visiting; and some of them should assume a continuity of activity.

These areas are made the basis of a question in the sociometric test, and are called *criteria* for association.

Each question is so framed that the individual is asked to name a limited number of people from within the group with whom he *would* choose to associate on the basis of each criterion.

It should be noted that a sociometric criterion should be stated in the conditional mood. The question is not "With whom do you associate?" but rather one that implies "If all things were possible and you could associate with anyone you liked, with whom would you choose to associate?"

The choices are usually limited to three or four on each criterion. To require more makes the task psychologically difficult for the individual and his answers become less meaningful and less decisive.

How Many Criteria and Choices to Use

It has been customary for each investigator to design his own sociometric test. Provided he knows the group and can select criteria which are appropriate to it, this is a wise procedure. How many criteria and choices to allow is, however, rather difficult to determine. Statistically, the greater the number of criteria and the more choices allowed proportionate to the number of individuals making up the group, the greater the probability of each person being chosen, but in actuality this does not happen. Psychologically, increased criteria and choices increase the difficulty of the task. With two-year-old children, one or two choices are the most that will be named. As age increases more and more names can be given. It is possible to allow "as many names as you wish." Statistical methods can be adjusted to deal with this, but psychologically, scores based on chance expectancy become confused (see section 4), for the question arises whether the individual should expect to receive as he gives. That is, should those who make more choices expect to receive more?

Example 1

Example 1 : SOCIOMETRIC TEST FOR GRADES 4–8

Name .... Date .... Room ....
1. When you are playing at recess which children in this classroom would you like best to play with you?
    1st choice .... 2nd choice .... 3rd choice ....
2. When you are working on a project in your class which children would you like best to work with you?
    1st choice .... 2nd choice .... 3rd choice ....
3. If you are having a party, which children from this classroom would you invite to it?
    1st choice .... 2nd choice .... 3rd choice ....

Criteria have ranged in number from one (1) to eight (2) or more, and choices from one to "as many as you like." Often neither experimental evidence nor rational explanation is given to justify the number. However, it has been suggested that the criteria should cover wide areas and different aspects of life within the group, and that the number of choices should be that which the individuals will make without undue urging.

Meanwhile, until evidence is brought to support another plan, we suggest that for usual sociometric situations *tests using three criteria and allowing three choices be used.*[*] By using the same number of criteria and choices the results are more directly comparable without further statistical adjustment. Using the identical wording for tests given to different groups within the same general category is advisable provided the criteria have the *same meaning* to the different groups. That is, the criterion of "playing in the garden" on our nursery school form may be conveniently used in other nursery schools provided they offer this type of play. However it is wiser to re-word the criteria to suit the exact situation, than to use those which are available simply because they have been used by other investigators.

Use of Last Choices

In early forms of the sociometric test "negative" choices were included; that is, each individual was asked to state which members of the group he would like least to associate with. This was useful, in that it enabled one to distinguish between those who were simply not chosen (neglectees) and those who were actively rejected by the group. However this item has been deleted from most sociometric tests because it was found to cause resentment and comment in the group;

---

[*]Samples of those we have used for nursery school, grade schools, high schools and camps are given on page 7.

Criteria used in sociometric tests at the Institute of Child Study University of Toronto

Nursery School and Kindergarten (asked verbally and individually)

1. What do you like to play with in the garden?
Who do you like to do that with best? Who else? Who else?
2. What do you like to do in the playroom? Who do you like to do that with best? Who else? Who else?
3. Who do you like to sit beside in the music circle? Who else? Who else?
(Note the form of the criteria is changed from the conditional with this young group.)

(a) *Elementary School*—Grades 4 to 8 (group test; prepared blanks with space for three choices on each criterion)

1. Suppose you were to move to another classroom, which boys and girls from this classroom would you like best to go with you?
2. Which boys or girls of this classroom would you like best to play with you during recess?
3. What do you like to do best in school? .... Write the names of the boys and girls in this classroom you would like best to do it with you.
4. What do you like doing out of school? .... Which boys and girls from *any* classroom would you like best to do it with you?
(Score only the first three questions. The fourth is to be used as a clue to children's relations outside the class.)

(b) *Secondary School*

1. Suppose you were to move to another classroom, which boys and girls from this classroom would you like best to go with you?
2. Suppose you were going away on a summer holiday, who from this classroom would you like to go with you?
3. Suppose you were going on a class outing. Each car holds four people. Who from this classroom would you like to have in your car?
4. Suppose you were going to a game—hockey, or football, or basketball or any game—who from this class would you choose to go with you?

Camps

1. If you were arranging your own cabin-group, which campers would you like to have in it with you?
2. If you were going on an out-trip for several days, which campers would you like to go with you?
3. When you go home from camp and are told you may invite any three campers to spend a week-end with you, which ones will you ask?
(Note: This is designed for use in boys' or girls' camps; for co-educational camps other criteria will have to be devised.)

also rejection scores were most peculiarly distributed statistically (3); and in so far as most people are not actively interested in those with whom they do *not* associate, the question itself was artificial.

However, by combining the rejections and acceptances that individuals receive, different personality "types" become apparent. Thus:

(a) High Acceptance and High Rejection—the dynamic contro-versial person: often a public figure.

(b) High Acceptance and Low Rejection—the well-liked person with appeal for the group, often a leader usually supportive of and abetting the group's values.

(c) Low Acceptance and High Rejections—antagonistic to and disruptive of the group values, unsupportive.

(d) Low Acceptance and Low Rejection—a non-descript, incon-spicuous personality; often withdrawn or recessive.

A valid sociometric score cannot be obtained simply by subtracting rejections from acceptances. This has been done in some studies, but obviously an individual who receives 20 acceptances and 20 rejections and by this formula obtains a score of zero is not sociometrically comparable to an individual who receives no acceptances and no rejections and by this formula would receive the same score.

In the ordinary routine test we suggest omitting "last choices." For particular researches, they should, of course, be used (4).

References

1. BYRD, EUGENE. "A Study of Validity and Constancy of Choices in a Sociometric Test." *Sociometry*, Vol. XIV (1951), Nos. 2–3.

2. LOEB, NORA. "The Educational and Psychological Significance of Social Acceptability and its Appraisal in an Elementary School Setting." Unpub-lished Ph.D. thesis, University of Toronto, 1941.

3. NORTHWAY, MARY L. *Appraisal of the Social Development of Children at a Summer Camp.* pp. 48ff. University of Toronto Studies, Psychology Series, Vol. V (1940), No. 1.

4. KIDD, JOHN W., "An Analysis of Social Rejection in a College Men's Residence Hall." *Sociometry*, Vol. XIV (1951), Nos. 2–3, 226–34. Reprinted in *The Sociometry Reader*, pp. 428–36.

3
How to administer the test

THE TEST may be given to a whole group at once or to each person individually.

Individual Testing

For children below grade 4, it is essential to give the test to each child individually and record the answers for him. The tester will have to be astute in developing good rapport before asking the questions. With nursery school children, the adult simply introduces the question as part of an apparently informal conversation. The test may also be given to older subjects individually. It is especially desirable to give it when it is possible to include sociometric questions with other tests, or as part of a fuller interview. Whenever a sociometric test is administered to subjects individually, all members of the group should be given it within as short a time as possible, so that chance for discussion among them is lessened.

Group Testing

Preliminary instructions are given to the group, and prepared question forms distributed. These are completed as quickly as possible and they are collected immediately. The whole procedure, in a classroom situation, takes about fifteen minutes. With adult subjects some investigators simply provide each with a blank paper and read the questions to them. This reduces the feeling of "test or examination," but increases incompleteness of answer and difficulty of scoring the papers.

Preliminary Instructions

It is important that everyone in the group should have an understanding of why the test is being given. The initial instructions must provide an explanation that is satisfying, serious, and if possible, should suggest that the stated choices are going to be carried out in actual re-organization of the group. The instructions should be clear and brief. Opportunities for questions should be allowed. The need for subjects to fill in each blank on the sheet should be emphasized.

It is fairly simple to devise instructions from which children will readily and honestly answer the questions. However, with adolescents and adults such inquiries often seem impertinent. The investigator must be ingenious in overcoming the resistance engendered by the tests' impact on established folkways expressed at least sub-vocally as

Example 2

FOR CHILDREN 12 TO 16 AT A SUMMER CAMP

"At camp, you like to do lots of things with other campers. In order to help the staff work out your groups we would like you to tell us which campers you would like best to do things with. We'd like to know who you would like to cabin with, to go on a canoe trip with, to be in your favorite activity with. *When we know these things, we will try to work out the groups the way you'd like them to be.*" (The statement in italics must not be used unless it is intended to put sociometric preferences into actual effect.) "So we are asking you to answer a few questions. One question is 'Who of all the campers would you most like to go on a canoe trip with?' Put down the name of the camper you'd most like to go with you. Then the name of the camper you'd choose second and then the name of the one you'd choose third. Another is 'Who would you like to cabin with you?' Are there any questions? Be sure to fill in each space."

"It's not proper to have preferences," or "It's none of his d——— business" or "How are they going to use this against me?" Examples of types of instructions and questions used in a variety of situations are to be found in articles in *Sociometry* (1, 2, 3, 4). While these articles can be used to suggest instructions and criteria for a test, it is imperative that the investigator know thoroughly the situation in which he is working and so can formulate preliminary instructions and an actual test form which will be acceptable and appropriate for the particular situation.

(NOTE: If the subjects have been informed that the results will be kept confidential, they must be kept confidential! They *should* be in any case.)

The question of *absentees* frequently arises. If individuals belonging to the group are absent it is possible for them to receive choices but not to give them. This throws out the statistical balance and possibly affects the absentee's true score. Give the test therefore when as many members of the group are present as possible. If an absentee returns to the group within a week's time give him the test individually immediately on his return and include his choices with the others.

Who should administer the test has been given very little consideration. It is certainly a point to be studied by research. Until a scientifically validated answer is reached, our suggestion is that it should be given by the person who can convey to the group a plausible and acceptable explanation for being asked all these questions by him.

NOTE ON STATISTICS: It is important that every individual fill in all the choices required on every criterion. If more than one per cent of the total number of choices of the whole group are not completed, statistical adjustments will have to be made. However, an individual must not be forced to complete his test form. If he does not make a choice after once being urged by "be sure to fill in every blank" or some similar phrase he probably cannot. It is easier to adjust the statistics than the psychological falsity of forced statements.

References

1. COOPER, D. H. "The Potentialities of Sociometry for School Administration." *Sociometry*, Vol. X (1947), No. 2, 111–21.

2. LUNDBERG, C. A., HERTZLER, V. B., DICKSON, L. "Attraction Patterns in a University." *Sociometry*, Vol. XII (1949), No. 2, 1–58.

3. MAUCORPS, PAUL H. "A Sociometric Inquiry in the French Army." *Sociometry*, Vol. XII (1949), No. 1, 46–80.

4. SCHAUER, GERHARD. "Social Adjustment in a Mental Hospital Community." *Sociometry*, Vol. IX (1946), Nos. 2–3.

4

How to organize the results

THE FOLLOWING METHOD of organizing the results is suggested because it includes each item of the original data and enables the total information to be arranged on one sheet.

Preparing a Summary Sheet or Sociometric Matrix

Prepare a large summary sheet, preferably on cardboard, and pin it to a drafting board. Rule horizontal and vertical columns; three more columns than the number of individuals in the group are needed. Enter the individuals' names alphabetically along the top and down both sides.

If there are distinct sub-groups that choose each other relatively infrequently such as boys and girls in public school classrooms, or sub-groups which you wish to study separately, such as Jews and Protestants in a club enter their names alphabetically but separately on the summary sheet. When this summary sheet is completed it forms a matrix of sociometric scores.

Filling the Summary Sheet

Arrange the test sheets in alphabetical order. From each test form note on each criterion the choices which have been made. For each choice received score 1.* If *Adams* has chosen *Brown* on the first criterion enter a 1 in the horizontal column beside Adams' name and in the vertical column under Brown. If he has not chosen him on the second enter a zero and if he has chosen him on the third enter a 1. Thus the square under Brown's name and beside Adams' will read 101. Do this for each test form. Be sure every choice made has been entered. If Allan has not chosen Adams on any criteria one may leave the square blank. This gives more clarity than entering the three zeros.

Obtaining the Scores

When the summary sheet is completed:

1. By adding each vertical column the number of choices each individual received on each criterion is obtained. Enter this in the column "Totals—On each criterion." Add these together and enter in the

---

*Our students prefer entering 1, 2, or 3, depending on whether the person has received a first, second, or third choice, but adding them as if each had the value of one. For this alternate method, see *Sociometric Testing: A Guide for Teachers.*

column "Totals—Combined." This is his *social acceptance* score or *choice-status*, or *sociometric status*.

2. Count the number of different people who have chosen an individual. Enter this in the column "Number choosing." This will be his *social receptiveness* score.

3. Count the number of different individuals whom he has chosen by counting the entries in the horizontal column. Enter this in the column "Number chosen." This is his *emotional expansion* score.

Example 3

FIGURATIVE SUMMARY SHEET OF SOCIOMETRIC SCORES

Date—*Nov. 7, 1951*   Group—*Rm. 7, Smith's School*

Boys	Adams	Brown	Dodds	Fatt	GIRLS	Allan	Best	Edwds.	Grand	Number Chosen
Adams, J.	—	PR (101)	100	←						2
Brown, Bob	001	—		010		010				3
Dodds, Jim	(011)		—							1
Fatt, P.	→(101)		010	—						2
GIRLS										
Allan, J.						—	R (111)	001		2
Best, Mary						R 111	—		010	2
Edwds., Maud						→(011)	—		001	2
Grand, D.						100			—	1
TOTALS On each criterion	113	101	110	010		221	122	001	011	
Combined	5	2	2	1		5	5	1	2	
Number choosing	3	1	2	1		3	2	1	2	

Types of Relationships

1. Look along the line opposite each individual's name and *encircle* the highest number(s) of choices given to any one person, provided this is a score of more than one. This gives the individual's *preferred companion.*

2. Look along the line opposite the name of the preferred companion. If his highest number of choices goes to the person who chose him most, the two form a *reciprocated* pair ("friends"). Indicate this by putting an R in both the squares where their columns meet.

3. From the summary sheet other relationships may be filled in as follows:

(*a*) Partially reciprocated choices. Enter PR where an individual choice is responded to by a choice of less value.

(*b*) One-way choices. Enter → where a person's choice is not reciprocated at all.

For a modified form of sociometric matrix, see Northway and Weld, 1957. (1)

The Social Atom

If from the summary sheet the names of all the individuals a person chooses and all those who choose him are listed and if each choice is noted as "reciprocated," "partially reciprocated," "one-way choice," etc., is entered, a summary of the individual's complete social relationships will be obtained. This is the individual's *social atom.*

Reference

1. Northway, Mary L. and Weld, Lindsay. *Sociometric Testing: A Guide for Teachers.* Toronto: University of Toronto Press, 1957.

5
What to do with the scores

THE INFORMATION on the summary sheet may be used as a basis from which to organize the sociometric scores, to investigate the various relationships between individuals, and to discover the structure of the group as a whole. In this section we shall deal with organizing the scores. The scores on the summary sheet are the actual number of choices an individual receives and gives. What should be done with them further depends on *the purpose for which the material is to be used.*

This is the point at which confusion often enters, because the investigator becomes unnecessarily bewildered by the bogey "statistics." A point to remember is that the score as it stands is the *result of the particular test and the group in which it was given.* For example, a child in a kindgarten of 15 children on a test using two questions and one choice, might get a score of 25. Another child in a kindgarten of 50 children on a test using five questions and one choice might also get a score of 25. But these scores do not mean the same thing, for in the first case the child is chosen by almost every one in his class on both questions. In the second, he is chosen 25 times out of a possible 245* times he could have been chosen. It is because every score is a function of the conditions under which it was obtained that further manipulation of the scores is necessary.

The Purpose for Which the Material is to be Used

1. To discover the sociometric state of affairs for one group on one occasion.

A teacher or camp director gives the test to his group because he wants to know which children are accepted by the others, which are not, which are friends, and so on. The material on the summary sheet itself will give him this information. He can see some children receive no choices, others a great many. In order to clarify this information it is helpful to list the individuals in rank order according to their scores.

From this he can see how the children vary in sociometric status at that particular time. As actual rank may not be very significant—that is, a person with a rank of 10 may have almost the same score as the persons with the ranks of 11, 12, 13—and as a rank of 10 in a group of 10 is different from a rank of 10 in a group of 50, it is convenient to

*245 rather than 250 because he cannot choose himself.

talk about the individuals according to what part of the rank order they belong. The list of names may be divided into equal parts, such as halves, quarters, tenths, etc., and a line drawn across the list to show where each division comes. Then we can designate an individual as being in the highest quarter (quartile),* or lowest tenth (decile) of the group.

The teacher will find it useful to divide the scores this way if he wishes to compare children who are in the different sections of sociometric status on some other characteristic such as their age, school marks, sports ability, and so on, or to discover whether in a Jewish-Gentile group there are proportionately more Jewish children at one sociometric level than there are at another.

Example 4

INDIVIDUALS ON SOCIOMETRIC TEST GIVEN AT .... ON .... ARRANGED IN RANK ORDER (Total number in group 40)

Name	Score	Rank	Reciprocated Choices
John Jones	30	1	
Mary Smith	28	2	
Maud Winters	23	3	
Jessie Brown	23	3	
Pete James	18	5	
Alice Bray	1	39	
George Watson	0	40	

---

2. To compare the sociometric status of individuals in the same group on two or more occasions using the same form of the test.

A teacher may wish to discover how the sociometric status of children changes over a week, month, or year. By giving a second test and ranking the children he may compare results with those on the first and see which children have gone up in rank and which down and by how many places.

A rank correlation coefficient $1 - \dfrac{6\Sigma d^2}{n(n^2-1)}$ will give the constancy of the rank order. The coefficient will be expected to become lower the longer the period between the two tests. (See section on reliability.)

This method of ranking and division into quarters is probably all

*The quartile is actually the point on the scale above which one quarter of the scores fall.

that is necessary for many practical investigations. It has, however, certain weaknesses, the chief of which is this. A child on two tests might have the highest score, therefore his rank would be *one* on each occasion. However, the scores of the group on the first test might range from zero to thirty, on the second from five to fifteen. His rank remains the same although his score has changed. Ranking takes no account of the distribution of scores, only their relative position.

The inadequacy of using either the actual score an individual obtains or his rank in a group becomes more apparent in the following type of study.

3. To compare the sociometric scores which have been obtained in groups of different sizes and/or on tests using a different number of criteria or choices.

For example we may want to compare a child's sociometric status in his classroom group of fifty with that in his club of twenty children, or we may want to discover the difference in sociometric scores of thirty workers in an industry from those of eighty children at a summer camp, or to compare the sociometric attributes of a group functioning under democratic conditions with those of one under autocratic leadership.

To compare the sociometric facts of unequalized groups it is necessary to develop some frame of reference by which a score obtained in one group can be compared with a score obtained in a different one. An absolute criterion which is independent of the phenomena of the particular test is necessary.

The absolute criterion described by Bronfenbrenner (1) is based on defining the scores obtained on a sociometric test in terms of the probability of obtaining them if chance alone were operating under the given mathematical conditions. Thus each raw score may be transformed into its probability of chance occurrence. A raw score of 15 on one test might be obtained by chance alone. 01; in another situation a raw score of 15 may be obtained by chance .40.* By using probability measures, scores obtained in any test may be compared with those obtained on any other. The mathematical factors of the size of the group, number of criteria, number of choices are made constant and what actual differences occur may be accounted for by what may be called social and psychological forces.

Fortunately for the investigator who wishes to be spared the task of working out probabilities for a given sociometric situation there are two available aids.

(a) If he is working with a typical group ranging in size from 20 to 50 individuals, using a test employing from one to three criteria with

*For readers unfamiliar with the statistics of probability, these figures mean that the scores would be expected once in a hundred times or 40 in 100 times were chance operating alone,

one to five choices on each, by consulting Bronfenbrenner (1, p. 71) he will find a table showing the raw score values which occur at the probability levels of .50 and .01. These are the arbitrary points at which Bronfenbrenner has established his limits of "above average," "significantly above average," "below average," and "significantly below average."

(b) If he is working with an atypical group in terms of size, or in terms of the character of the sociometric test being used, then critical levels should be developed, taking into account these peculiar characteristics. Also in some cases, although working with typical groups, the experimenter will wish to discriminate more than four levels of significance, and here, too, the levels must be generated from the basic characteristics of the sociometric situation. Fortunately, the work involved can be greatly reduced by referring to tables which give close approximations of the terms of any binomial that must be expanded to determine the probability attached to the various scores for any particular sociometric situation. Bronfenbrenner gives instructions for using Salvosa's (2) tables in sociometric testing. Later developments on use of the matrix are given in Reference 5.

Some Idiosyncracies of Sociometric Scoring

1. Statistical equivalence of score and psychological difference of choice.

In the statistical procedures we have described, it is tacitly accepted that all choices are of equal value. Psychologically, it is not necessarily so. This can be demonstrated most clearly by an absurd example. Suppose in a young people's club the question used was "Whom from this group would you like most to marry? Second choice? Third choice?" Obviously one young man might say "No one," and if forced to answer would select names with an attitude of "I don't care." Another young man's first choice might be of great psychological intensity and his others completely meaningless. While actual sociometric tests do not employ such drastic criteria, some variation of intensity of choice is undoubtedly present.

One attempt to take this factor of difference in intensity into account was to give weights of say 5. 3. 1 to a first, second, and third choice. This was criticized as being arbitrary; it was discontinued, however, because it complicated the statistics (1), and because it was found that weighted scores had a very high correlation (3) with unweighted ones. Undoubtedly the unweighted scores offer great statistical advantage; it must be remembered, however, that to consider each choice statistically equivalent, in terms of psychological factors is in itself an arbitrary decision.

The possibility is that the sociometric test itself will not provide an answer to the problem of personal intensity in human relations. This will have to be investigated through other measures. The problem of intensity is not unique to sociometry; some of the studies of attitude measurement may be found to give a lead towards a solution.

2. Equivalence of sociometric status of two or more individuals and difference in their influence in the group.

In a camp group two children may each receive choices which give them a score "slightly below chance." Yet their power in the group may vary. Child A may obtain his score because he is chosen by three of the most popular children in the group; and child B because he is chosen three times by one child who is himself isolated.

Suppose child C is chosen once by both A and B. Obviously the amount of social power he obtains from the choice made by A is greater than that he obtains from B, because A's vote is backed by his relation to powerful people and B is backed by one child who does not matter to the group.

A method of calculating the weight of the choice made by an individual in terms of the weight of the scores he himself received is described by Katz (4). This defines a person's sociometric status in terms of the *power* he sways in the group.

The most important thing for the teacher or research worker to remember is this: Statistics are made for science and not science for statistics. Select those statistical methods which will most adequately help organize your data and enable them to be used. Statistics form a most important tool; they do not atone, however, for inadequate data. And, too, in no other area is it so easy to misrepresent the facts by inappropriate statistical analyses than in that of sociometry. Some sociometric findings which are publicly quoted are to be mistrusted until evidence of the statistics used is given. Published articles are on the whole trustworthy, because the statistical methods which have been employed are usually described in full.

References on the Statistics of Sociometry

1. BRONFENBRENNER, URIE. *The Measurement of Sociometric Status, Structure and Development.* Sociometry Monograph No. 6, Beacon House, 1945. Previously published in *Sociometry*, Vol. VI (1943), No. 4; Vol. VII (1944), No. 1. All students using sociometry for research purposes, and all workers conducting investigations which require comparison of different sociometric tests should consult this work. The previous articles on statistical problems arising in sociometry are given as references in this monograph. The student who wishes to pursue the problem further should consult subsequent issues of *Sociometry* in which he will find articles extending, clarifying, and criticizing this method of approach.

2. SALVOSA, L. R. *Generalizations of the Normal Curve of Error.* Ann

Arbor, Michigan: Edwards Bros., Inc., 1930.

3. FRANKEL, ESTHER. "The Social Relationships of Pre-School Children." *Sociometry*, Vol. IX (1946), Nos. 2–3, and Sociometry Monograph No. 11. See p. 19.

4. KATZ, LEO. "A New Status Index Derived From Sociometric Analysis." *The Sociometry Reader*, Glencoe: Free Press (1960), pp. 266–71.

5. See also articles in *The Sociometry Reader*, Glencoe: Free Press (1960), by Edwards, Forsyth, Katz, Festinger, Criswell, Zeleny.

6

The reliability and validity of a sociometric test

THE USUAL MEASURES of reliability and validity do not seem to be particularly appropriate for sociometry. Other tests such as those of intelligence and personality are based on the assumption that they are measuring a factor, capacity, or trait within the individual. Sociometry, however, is concerned with discovering the preferred relationships which are present in a group at a particular time. If each individual discloses his preferences on the test honestly, the test is perfectly reliable and valid.

In working out measures of reliability, the more usual psychological tests assume that they are measuring a trait which remains constant and that if the scores vary this reflects inadequacies of the test rather than changes in the characteristic. Therefore the correlation of the scores obtained on the test given on two occasions was taken as a measure of reliability. Sociometry, however, is based on the assumption that social preferences change, and indeed that by arranging fortuitous situations we may bring about changes we consider desirable. For example it was believed that by improving social conditions a teacher can help a child with a low score become more fully accepted by the group.

Another measure of reliability on usual tests is obtained by intercorrelating the scores on different test items. This assumes that all items are measures of the same factor or trait. Sociometry however does not assume a priori that a person chosen on one criterion (item) will be chosen also on another. Indeed, an investigator may set up sociometric criteria on which he expects different people to be chosen. For example Jennings (1) has devised a test using criteria from which she finds two types of social relations can be measured. These she calls acceptance in the psyche-group and in the socio-group.

There is yet another peculiarity in sociometric testing. An individual's score could be the same on two tests, yet his relationships might have changed completely. For example an individual in a group of 40 on the first test receives a score of 20. This is made up of one choice from 20 members of the group. On the second test he might also receive a score of 20 made up of choices from people who did not choose him at all on the first test. Thus a perfect reliability coefficient based on correlating scores on two tests (or scores from different criteria) could be obtained although all the actual choices made differed.

When we consider the question of *validity* other peculiarities arise. The validity of most psychological tests is measured by checking the test results with some outside measure. So tests of personality are checked against clinician's judgments of the individual's personality and tests of intelligence against actual performance of intellectual skills. In sociometry however the question asked is not "With whom do you associate?" but "With whom would you like to associate, all associations being possible?" The usual outside measures of validity can at best appraise what associations are actually formed and are as a rule inadequate to determine what associations are wished for. Theoretically, it would be possible to have a social situation in which no stated preference was found in actual practice, and yet the sociometric test would not be invalid. For example, a test might ask children "With whom would you like to ride in a car to the sportsmeet?"; yet the adults who arranged the cars could make sure that not one choice was found in the actual situation.

Considering all these reasons for not expecting sociometric results to meet the usual measures of reliability and validity, the amazing thing is that when such measures are applied to these data relatively high coefficients are discovered. The next sections will discuss what some of the findings have been.

Reliability

1. *Correlations between different test-items.* Loeb's correlations on odd-even items in 12 classrooms ranged from .65 to .85 and on split-halfs of the test from .53 to .85.

The present author obtained correlations of .64 to .84 between *general* criteria and .37 to .50 between criteria based on particular skills and those on general factors.

Jennings, relating scores on criteria designed to discover psyche-group relationships with those set up to measure socio-group relationships, obtained correlations of .4 to .5 (1).

Indeed, in the literature we have been unable to discover any negative correlations of significance. It would appear that the more general the criteria the higher the correlations between them; the more specific the lower the correlations become.

This suggests that if factor analysis were applied to sociometric results one might discover factors comparable to Spearman's G and s. That is, there might be a P factor standing for Personality quality that underlies acceptance and s factors which imply qualities for acceptance in situations requiring particular skills or characteristics.

2. *Correlations between scores on tests given at different times.* The

"reliability coefficient" obtained by correlating the scores from repeated tests generally drops as the interval between the tests increases. With nursery and primary grade children, these may be as high as .79 for a week's interval, but drop to .63 for an eight-week interval. A coefficient of .74 was obtained for a three-week interval with camp adolescents (2) and of .65 after an eight-month interval with girls in a training home (1). However, despite the length of interval, the correlations remain positive. In fact, tests from school groups given two years apart correlated .5 (in file), and from day care children a year apart, .39. The correlations from tests given after a long interval are based on scores of only the residue of cases remaining in the group through the period. That is, as many as 50 per cent of the original members of the group have left and been replaced by newcomers. These facts again suggest that the test is measuring some factor other than it superficially appears to seek.

In recent studies, scores obtained by children on sociometric tests from nursery school to Grade 6, that is, over a nine year period, have been correlated. The significance levels are .001 to .05 for correlations between tests two to three years apart; with increasing intervals the significance drops. However, scores in kindergarten predict scores in fifth grade at the .01 level (paper in preparation). These more recent studies use product–moment correlations and are handled by computer programming. Raw sociometric scores have been found to yield better correlations than transformed scores when two or more sets of sociometric scores are correlated. When sociometric scores are correlated with scores on other measures, it appears that transformed scores are better. (See the section on distribution of sociometric scores.)

3. *Constancy of choice.* Another method of measuring reliability is by ascertaining how many of the actual preferences stated on the first test are repeated on a later one. In our camp study we found 66 per cent of the first choices made on the first test, were repeated three weeks later on the second test; 50 per cent of second choices and 35 per cent of third were repeated. The correlation between the sociometric scores on two tests was .69 (2).

This suggests that an investigation might be made to discover the relationship between consistency in sociometric status and variation in the choices from which status is formed.

It also suggests that the percentage of choices at each level remaining over a period of time might indicate a way of weighting the scores if not in terms of "intensity" at least of durability.

Considering the many natural and consciously planned factors that we assume influence social status, it is noteworthy that such a degree of consistency of status is maintained over such long intervals. There is some evidence that the consistency of status in children's groups increases with age (2, 3).

The question of measuring the reliability of a test seems to be ignored in many studies. As a general rule, it is suggested that the investigator, using a test for the first time, should work out the inter-correlations of scores obtained on each criterion of his test and also, if possible, repeat the test on the same population within a maximum of ten days.

Validity

The validity of a test is usually determined by checking its results against some other measure of the same quality. An assumption has been made that sociometric scores and actual social contacts should show a high degree of agreement. While two such measures do show positive correlation of around .5, one should not assume that the sociometric results are validated or invalidated by lack of correspondence in actual contacts. Sociometry asks with whom you would *like* to associate, all associations being possible. Actual contacts are influenced by the exigencies of the situation, such as the amount of external control, area in which contacts are made, placement of equipment, conventions of the group, and characteristics such as hesitancy, shyness, or domination, that determine the actual contact.

An interesting study of reliability and validity was made by Eugene Byrd (4), in which sociometric choice was correlated with actual choice made on the identical criterion. A sociometric test was given to fourth-grade children. It used one criterion, "Who would you like to be in a play with you?" During the next eight weeks each child was allowed to choose his companions and put on an actual play in the classroom. After the eight weeks, the original test was repeated. The correlations were: Test I and actual companions .76; actual companions and Test II, .80; Test I and Test II, .89. The differences in the correlations are not statistically significant. It should be noted that validity of choice measured against actual selection on the *identical criterion* is remarkably high. This study gives a clue to how further measures of validity might be made.

Another method of judging validity is to relate scores to some outside judgment. This has been carried out in sociometry several times. A rather extensive investigation by Gronlund (5) discovers that 40 sixth-grade teachers' judgments of the sociometric status of children in their classrooms correlates from .26 to .83, mean .59, with actual status. The conditions under which greatest and least discrepancies occur are analysed. Gronlund shows that this judgment method of establishing validity is tenuous, because the judges are influenced, among other things, by the preferences they themselves have among their pupils. The most comprehensive accounts of the reliability and validity of sociometric scores are by Mouton, Blake, and Fruchter; these appeared in the journal *Sociometry* in 1955 and are reprinted in

The Sociometry Reader. (6)

The facts we have outlined show that the usual measures of reliability and validity result always in positive and often in high coefficients. This suggests that the tests are measuring something more than they purport to do. They may be designed only to measure the preferences present in a group at one time but they seem to be locating some underlying factor that is expressed in the different choices. A question arises similar to the one raised about intelligence tests years ago. What is the test measuring? It is probable that during the next decade sociometrists will give as many different answers as the "mental testers" have. It is to be hoped, however, they will bypass the classic *cul-de-sac*: "The intelligence test measures intelligence; intelligence is what the intelligence test measures."

References

1. JENNINGS, HELEN H. *Leadership and Isolation*, pp. 51, 252. New York: Longmans, Green and Co., 1950.

2. NORTHWAY, MARY L. *Appraisal of the Social Development of Children at a Summer Camp*, pp. 31, 35, 39, 40, 74. University of Toronto Studies, Psychology Series, Vol. V (1940), No. 1.

3. FRANKEL, ESTHER B. "The Social Relationships of Pre-School Children." *Sociometry*, Vol. IX (1946), Nos. 2–3, 21.

4. BYRD, EUGENE. "A Study of Validity and Constancy of Choices in a Sociometric Test." *Sociometry*, Vol. IX (1946), Nos. 2–3, 21.

5. GRONLUND, N. *Accuracies of Teachers' Judgments Concerning the Sociometric Status of Sixth Grade Pupils*. Sociometry Monograph No. 25. Beacon, New York: Beacon House, 1951.

6. MOUTON, JANE S., BLAKE, R. R., and FRUCHTER, B. "The Reliability of Sociometric Measures and the Validity of Sociometry Measures," *The Sociometry Reader*, pp. 320–87. Glencoe: Free Press, 1960.

7

The target sociogram

Distributions of Sociometric Scores

The scores obtained from a sociometric test may be placed on a distribution graph with the number of cases in the ordinate, and the scores in intervals of raw scores, percentiles, or probability intervals on the abscissa. When this is done, it will be found that the distribution is skewed *positively*. That is, a greater number of cases is found in the lower intervals than in the middle or higher intervals. Figure 1 shows a typical distribution.

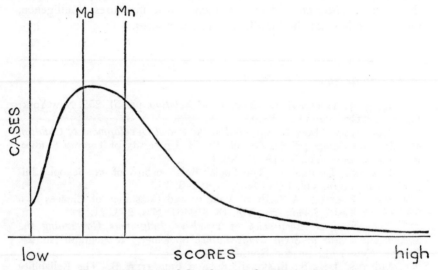

FIGURE 1. A typical distribution of sociometric scores.

An explanation of this particular form arises from the consideration of the following facts. The statistics of sociometry are such that an individual in a group of usual size is more likely not to be chosen than to be chosen by any other individual.* For example, if John X. in a group of 40 is allowed to make 9 choices on a test, the chances of George Y. being chosen by him are 9/39 and of not being chosen by him, 30/39.

The piling-up of cases in the lower intervals may result from the fact

*The sociometry of small groups, that is those composed of less than ten individuals, is not considered here. Obviously the chance of being chosen becomes greater the smaller the size of the group.

that the low scores are obtained by both the unliked and the rejected individuals. If last choices were used and these scores combined with the positive scores, it is probable that the distribution would be extended at the lower end.

It is probable that if each individual were allowed sufficient choices to enable him, by chance, to choose every member of the group, and if low scores were differentiated by using "last choices," the whole distribution would approximate a normal curve except at the upper end. The only explanation of the attenuation there seems to be is that a few individuals receive scores far beyond the expectations of chance, which probably reflects our cultural pattern of emphasizing "leader-ship"—"To him that hath, shall be given." For further discussion of these points the reader should read Moreno (1) on the *sociodynamic* effect, and the present author on the influences of the culture on social preferences (2).

Sociograms

There are many means of displaying sociometric facts and the choice of a particular method depends on the aspects of sociometric relations in which one is most interested. For depicting the social structure of an entire group, each individual's status in it, and the predominant relationships among these individuals, the *Target Socio-gram* offers a convenient method. This was designed by the present author (3) and improved by Bronfenbrenner, Quarrington (4), and others. Figures 2 and 3 show targets made up of data from actual situation, and ways by which the targets may be elaborated.

To make a target diagram, draw four concentric circles, the areas of each division being equal to one-quarter of the whole target. Depending on the scoring previously used, each circle may be used to represent the four quartiles or the four levels of probability, significantly above chance, above chance, below chance, and significantly below chance.

The individuals whose scores on the scoring sheet fall into these divisions may now be entered by name or initial in the appropriate division of the target. If a group is composed of the two sexes, males should be indicated by a small triangle, females by a small circle, and placed on opposite sides of the diagram.

By looking at the diagram at this point, one may observe each person's sociometric status in terms of his proximity to the center of circumference of the target.

Now looking at the record form again, note each individual's highest choice. Draw a line from his name on the target to the name of the person he chooses most often and place an arrow at the end of the line.

In the case of two people choosing each other more highly than they choose anyone else, draw a double headed arrow. Such a relationship is called a reciprocal choice.

Second highest choices, and indeed all choices may be entered in a similar manner. They will add valuable detail to the diagram, but will tend to reduce the clarity.

At this point the target will show the social status of the individuals, their predominating interpersonal relations, and the structure of the group as a whole.

Other Uses of the Target

1. To depict the sociograms of a community formed of two or more sub-groups (boys, girls; negro, white; etc.), the target may be segmented in the proportion of the sub-group in the total community; self-preference scores indicated; and inter-sub-group choices drawn (4).

This would seem to be a most useful tool in these days of concern about segregation and integration not only of the Negro–white groups in the United States, but in countries such as Canada, where large groups of immigrant children are attending the schools. Presumably high self-preference would be found in groups from different national backgrounds. It would be hoped that this would decrease with time as the schools develop language skills for communication among the groups and create classroom atmospheres in which the assets of the children from various backgrounds are appreciated. A useful device is to examine the target to see which children are choosing across the barriers and to make positive use of these cross-cultural relationships already in existence.

2. To depict the number of choices to or from a subject beyond his dominating ones which usually appear on the sociogram, place each subject on the target as usual, with a circle or triangle. Each additional outgoing choice is recorded by a small arrow outside his circle; these may point to the center of the target if they go to people of higher sociometric status; to the circumference if to individuals of lower sociometric status. Each choice coming to him is recorded similarly inside his circle. Thus his "emotional expansiveness" is depicted.

3. To compare two sociograms of the same group obtained at different times, it is useful to draw the second on transparent paper which can be superimposed on the original. The changes in each person's status and dominating choices can be readily compared.

While the target sociogram provides a means of depicting the sociometric findings clearly, the dangers of it have been discussed by the author in "a note on the use of target sociograms" (5). This article emphasizes the fact that the target is both an abstraction from the sociometric facts (which themselves are abstractions from the total

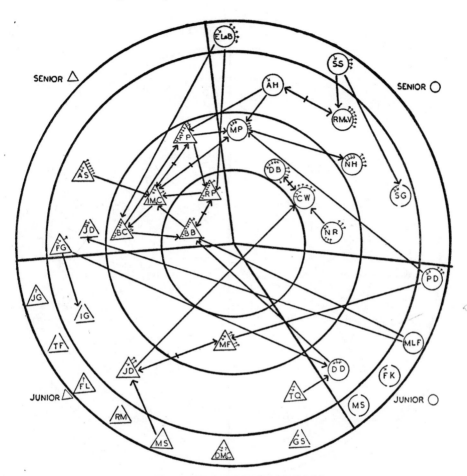

INSTITUTE NURSERY SCHOOL

FIGURE 2. This sociogram is of the Nursery School at the Institute of Child Study. The target is divided vertically into sections proportionate to the number of boys and girls in the school, and horizontally into junior and senior age groups. Each child is entered in the appropriate section according to his sociometric scores. Lines are drawn from each child to the person(s) he chooses most highly. Boys are represented by a triangle, girls by a circle; these are broken if the child was absent for the test and a question mark is entered in his symbol if he gives no adequate response. Small arrows within the circle indicate the number of other people who choose a child; those outside, the number of other people he chooses.

The position of so many juniors in the ouside circle suggests that two-year-olds are just beginning to be part of a sociometric structure. Seniors' positions for the most part are nearer the center; this reflects the fact that sociometric status at the nursery school level increases with age.

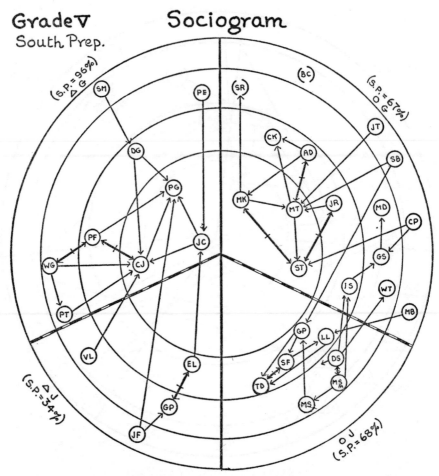

Grade V — South Prep. — **Sociogram**

FIGURE 3. This is a sociogram of a grade V classroom used in a study of Jewish-Gentile prejudice. The target was made in the usual way and divided vertically. It was then divided horizontally into sections proportionate to the number of Jewish and Gentile children in the group. Boys are placed to the left of the vertical line, girls to the right; Gentiles above the horizontal line and Jewish below; according to their sociometric status. Lines are drawn from each individual to the person(s) he chooses most often. Incompleted circles indicate the child was absent when the test was given.

It will be noted that this target shows complete sex cleavage in this age group. (Actually on the data sheet a few choices were made between the sexes.) The arrows crossing the horizontal lines show significant intercultural choices. The number outside each section gives the self-preference score of the sub-group calculated from the data sheet by Quarrington's method. For example the Jewish boys show a self-preference of 34 per cent; that is, they give 34 per cent more of their choices to each other than they would be expected to by chance.

social facts) and a symbol, which by suggesting the archery target implies erroneously that a "bull's eye" is the point of most worth.

Nevertheless, it amazes this author to see the extent to which the target sociogram has been used. It is reproduced widely in the sociometric literature and also in textbooks on child development both on this continent and abroad. It was an exciting experience last year to visit both Cardiff and Rome and to examine target sociograms from schoolrooms in Wales and Italy.

During the last fifteen years students taking the graduate diploma course at our Institute of Child Study have administered, scored and analysed sociometric tests and have been encouraged to draw sociograms which show the relationships and structure of each group as clearly as possible and at the same time reflect the students' creative and artistic skills. Figure 4 is a sociogram designed by Pat Grant, a recent student in this course.

Another form of the target sociogram was designed by Miss Dorothy McKenzie, supervisor of the Institute's nursery school. It is modelled on a child's peg board (see figure 5). Coloured pegs can be inserted in the appropriate position according to each child's score. Elastic bands are used to show reciprocal choices. By adjusting the pegs from one test to a later one of the same group, sociometric movement can be shown. Photographs taken of each peg board sociogram permit a permanent record to be made. The peg board sociograms in figure 5 show two groups of children who were in the same kindergarten in successive years. The contrast in the sociometric structure was clearly reflected in behaviour differences highly visible to the teacher. Group 1 was described as a difficult group, and group 2 as very pleasant in the classroom setting.

Indeed, the target sociogram has become such an integral part of our activities in Toronto, that when seeking a motif for the gates to our patio we even inveigled the architect to use the design of the target sociogram. The gate amuses our colleagues, but truly baffles the neighbours.

The target is useful as a "visual aid," but for detailed analyses of sociometric relations or for research work the total data from which it is abstracted should always be consulted.

References

1. MORENO, J. L. *Who Shall Survive? A New Approach to the Problem of Human Relationships.* Beacon, New York: Beacon House, 1934. Revised edition, 1953.

2. NORTHWAY, MARY L., FRANKEL, ESTHER, and POTASHIN, REVA. *Personality and Sociometric Status,* pp. 62 ff. Sociometry Monograph No. 11, 1947.

3. NORTHWAY, MARY L. "A Method for Depicting Social Relationships Obtained by Sociometric Testing." *Sociometry,* Vol. VIII (1940), No. 2, 144–50. Reprinted in *The Sociometry Reader,* pp. 221–26.

4. NORTHWAY, MARY L., and QUARRINGTON, BRUCE, "Depicting Intercultural Relationships." *Sociometry,* Vol. IX (1946), No. 4, 334–39.

5. NORTHWAY, MARY L. "A Note on the Use of the Target Sociogram." *Sociometry,* Vol. XIV (1951), No. 2–3, 235–36. Reprinted in *The Sociometry Reader,* pp. 227–28.

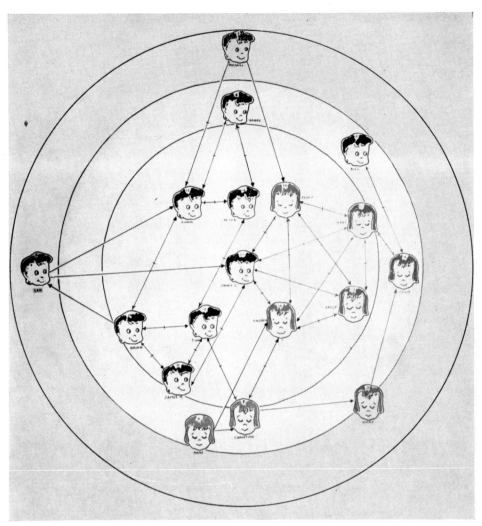

FIGURE 4 This is a student's sociogram of a Grade 1 group. It was selected for its artistry and clarity and also for its ingenious arrangement of relationships into geometric shapes. Note the pentagon made up of relationships among the boy in the centre and the four girls to the right; the triangle within a triangle at the top; the triangle of the outside boy on the left and his two companions nearer the centre; the two parallelograms—one of four boys to the left, the other (incomplete) from the centre boy with the boy and girls below him. Can you pick out the other geometric arrangements? Is there a geometry of sociometry?

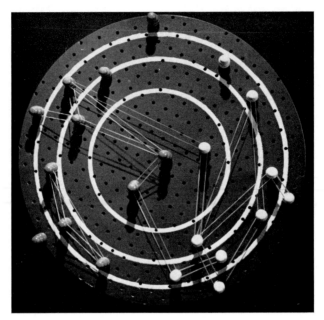

GROUP 1

FIGURE 5   THE PEG BOARD SOCIOGRAM

Note the target is divided into 4 equal areas. The pegs are placed to show the sociometric position of each individual. Identifying marks can be pasted on the top of each peg. The two groups shown are those of children in the same kindergarten in successive years. The difference in sociometric structure between two apparently similar groups was also reflected in the teacher's comments on the behaviour of the groups. Group 1 was described as "difficult," group 2 as "a pleasant group."

GROUP 2

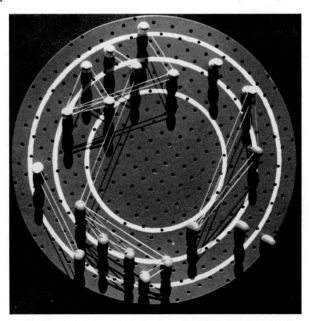

8
How to interpret the results

THE INFORMATION obtained from a sociometric test includes: (1) the sociometric status scores, their variation and distribution; (2) the relationships among the individuals in the group, the types of relationship and the classification of these into reciprocated choices, indifferents, one way choices, chains; (3) the structure of the group as a whole, which is discovered from the distribution of the scores and the relationships among the individuals.

Interpretation of the Sociometric Scores

What meaning has a sociometric status score beyond the fact that it states the number of choices the individual has received from members of that particular group? The usual interpretation given by the person who naively uses the test is one which reflects an assumption of our American culture, namely that the more a person possesses of wealth, fame, friends, the better he is (1). On this basis the interpretation is that the higher the sociometric status the better its possessor. The score is considered an index of social adjustment or indeed of mental health. Before we attempt to evaluate this interpretation, we will consider sociometric scores in three ways: first, the interpretation from an analysis of the scores themselves; second, the meaning of a score for other sociometric situations; and third, the relations of sociometric scores to other characteristics.

Interpretations from an analysis of the scores themselves. 1. A sociometric score is a gross unit, stating the total number of choices an individual receives. To interpret a gross score it should be refined into its components. *Scores which are statistically identical are rarely sociometrically equivalent.* On a given test three individuals may receive scores of nine. The first may have one choice from nine individuals all of whom are of higher sociometric status than himself and none of whom choose each other; the second from nine individuals all of lower sociometric status and few of whom choose each other; and the third three choices from three individuals of equal sociometric status, all of whom choose each other. Thus identical scores when analysed into their components will lead to different interpretations. Sociometric patterns may be of greater importance than sociometric scores in reaching an interpretation. Some studies have been made (2, 3, 4) but there is great need for further research to classify the patterns of the component parts which form a gross sociometric score.

In *Sociometric Testing: A Guide for Teachers* individual sociograms show differences in patterning and the changes in these over a time are given (5).

2. It should be noted that *on no usual sociometric test is any one individual chosen by every other member of the group, and also that only a few individuals are not chosen by any member of the group.* Individuals with a score of one or more are not isolates; they are chosen by someone. These facts are extremely important in developing an understanding of principles of social intercourse. It means that no one is actively liked by everyone and few people are unliked by everybody. The person popularly characterized as "universally liked" is not found sociometrically, and the person "nobody cares two hoots about" is a relatively rare individual.

In interpreting scores as "high" and "low," sometimes called leaders and isolates, it is important to keep the above facts in mind. It would be wise to look for which members of the group do *not* choose those with high scores and which members *do* choose those with low scores. Also it makes a difference in understanding a person's sociometric power to consider the sociometric status of the individuals who choose him. For example, an individual may be chosen by only two people and have a relatively low status, but if these two choosers have very high status, the individual may have a great deal of power in the group. He may well be "the power behind the throne" (6).

On many tests one or two individuals are found who receive a score of *zero*. Only such cases should spoken of as "isolates." It should be noted that if the test has not included *negative choices* the score of zero itself does not indicate whether the individual is ignored or actively disliked by the group.

Even in the cases which score zero it is doubtful whether isolate is the best term. For the individual himself has made his choices to members of the group, which gives him one-direction bonds in it. Probably the simpler term *"unchosen"* is more accurate. If an individual has a score of one or more, he is neither an isolate, nor unchosen; he has some relationship in the group. This also indicates the need to analyse in patterns of choice rather than make interpretations from gross scores.

⸳ *The generality of a sociometric score.* The question of whether a sociometric score is an index of a general trait of social acceptability has been discussed in the literature. But few studies focussed on this point have been made. Whether a score obtained in one group predicts the score which would be obtained in another would have to be determined by giving tests to different groups to which an individual belonged (his classroom, Sunday school, scouts, gang, etc.) and discovering the constancy of his status.

In 1947 we suggested an hypothesis that an individual's acceptance score as measured in one group is an index to what his acceptance score will be in a reasonably similar (cultural-age) group (7). So far as we know, no attempt has been made to verify this. However, as an addition to the data quoted at that time, we may state that a study of a group of 60 children from six to twelve years old in a day care centre was carried on over 12 months. During this period half of the children in the original group withdrew and were replaced by newcomers. Rank correlations of the status of children who were in the group on each of the two tests were calculated. It was found that after six months, 43 of the original children remained and their sociometric scores obtained in the whole group of 60 correlated .52 with those originally obtained; after a year 33 originals remained and the correlation was .39. As half the members of the total group had changed, the situation is somewhat comparable to taking measures in different groups with a 50 per cent overlap of membership. One therefore suspects that there is a tendency for an individual's sociometric status in one group to be positively related to his status in another similar group.

Indeed the recent studies from our own laboratory school, which we mentioned above, have investigated children's sociometric status over a period of several years. One study tracing sociometric status from Kindergarten to Grade III yielded a correlation of .89 between the scores of the ten children who remained in the group through the four years. Yet during this period eleven of the original children had left the group and six new ones had entered it. From these we have recently argued that there is a difference in social potential that is established in the very early years (8).

The studies now in preparation for publication have examined children's status over a period of nine years and show that it has a considerably high level of consistency, thus strengthening the notion of social potential.

The relation of sociometric scores to other characteristics. The question of what characteristics are related to sociometric scores arose early in the history of sociometry (9) and continues to be discussed in the current literature. The earliest approach was to search for factors related to sociometric status such as age, mental age, I.Q., academic skills, performance skills, socio-economic status, proximity of living, and ratings on personality tests. This was done either by correlating scores from the whole sociometric scale to the outside characteristic or by comparing the individuals grouped into high, middle, and low sociometric scores on outside characteristics. That these attempts led to rather inconclusive results is not surprising when the fact discussed above—variation of sociometric patterns underlying similar sociometric scores—is remembered. In most test situations such characteristics do not correlate highly or even positively with sociometric status.* However, there are exceptions. For example, when the age spread in a group is important in the social organization of the group, as in nursery schools and camps, some positive correlation may be found (10); competence in skills is related if the criteria of social acceptance are based on that skill (11). Personality questionnaire scores show some relation when the personality test used includes social items (12). Gronlund's *Sociometry in the Classroom* and Evans's *Sociometry in Education* discuss the relationship of sociometric status to other variables much more extensively.

Two of our series of studies give a clue to interpreting sociometric scores in terms of their relationship to other factors. One series was initiated by Loeb (13) in 1940. She discovered that children whose school achievement marks exceeded what would be expected on the basis of their mental age were higher in sociometric status than those whose achievement fell short of their mental age. This difference is statistically reliable. Loeb indicated that this implied that the child who has the skills the culture values is apt to be highly accepted. However, as the actual correlations between sociometric status and skills are for the most part low and the statistically significant finding is that the children whose achievement scores exceed those expected by their mental ability are higher in sociometric status, it is not the possession of the skill but the effort of the child in putting it to use that seems important. Our interpretation, therefore, was that "social acceptance is related to the degree and direction of a child's outgoing energy" (4). This hypothesis was investigated by the present author in a study of children of low sociometric status (4); it was possible to describe them either as lacking energy or as directing it against the welfare of the group. This was also supported by Hill (14) and has been substantiated by later studies including Baron (12). Two studies conducted in summer camps by Grapko (15) and Jourard (16) indicated that the child who expresses himself in terms of characteristics the group values, sportsmanship, fair play, etc. (15), and the child who directs his energy to the activities the group approves (16), are likely to be high in sociometric status.

These findings suggest that an individual's sociometric score reflects the extent to which he directs his effort towards actions which are valued by the cultural group that, through the test, is appraising him. It is therefore an index of the degree to which he attempts to conform

*Loeb's (11) correlations (r) in 12 classrooms between sociometric status and other characteristics were as follows: C.A.—.14 to .24; M.A.+.003 to .40; I.Q. —.17 to 30; arithmetic 13 to 63; social studies —.05 to .54; reading —.03 to .43.

to and abet the group's folkways and mores; in this sense it is a measure of his drive towards *external social adjustment.*

However, another series of studies should be considered. Studies which have compared sociometric scores with measures of inner personality patterns such as the Rorschach (17) and the Rosenzweig (18) have shown that indices of inner stress and insecurity are to be found at various levels of sociometric scores though in different forms. From these it would appear that children of middle sociometric status have better balance in their inner personality structure than those of very high or very low. Wigdor, from her study relating sociometric scores to Rorschach patterns, states:

The children who are high sociometrically on the Rorschach show a greater sensitivity to their environment—almost an active, conscious striving in using the feeling tone of a situation to further their own ends. They also include a strong need for affection. They tend to view situations in a conventional light. There is a conscious striving for approval. Those who have low sociometric scores are less able to control their emotions and seem a more egocentric, moody and impulsive group. They are often unable to react to a situation but nevertheless desire participation. There are proportionately more seriously disturbed individuals in the high and low sociometric groups than in the middle. In the high group the disturbances seem to be of psycho-neurotic origin or general anxiety, while in the low group there are schizo-phrenic or schizoid types of patterning (17).

Coons concludes from her study of the Rosenzweig in relation to sociometric status:

it might be suggested that the reactions of the child of intermediate status indicate certain trends with regard to frustration which are desirable from a mental hygiene standpoint. The "outsider" is apparently too socially insecure and afraid of failure to assert himself sufficiently. In the face of difficulty, he is patient and conforming. The "star" is perhaps so socially secure that it is unnecessary for him to either blame himself or exhibit concern for others (18).

This would suggest that the sociometric status should not be interpreted as a direct measure of adequacy of *personality structure* or *inner psychological health.*

These two sets of studies taken together suggest that gross sociometric status may be interpreted as an indication of the individual's external social adjustment to the values of the particular group, but that it does not reflect directly his degree of inner psychological *security* (19). It would seem that sociometric status is related to the individual's direction of energy to the goals of the group; the effort so made, however, may cause him inner stress and result in psychological imbalances. Possibly these relationships will be clarified when investigations give more attention to analysis of sociometric patterns, rather than to the mere gross score, and when further studies are made using projective tests to discover the difference they show between individuals of similar sociometric status.

From the above statements, we may suggest a few points to keep in mind when interpreting scores of sociometric status:

1. Individuals vary in gross sociometric status, but identical scores can only be interpreted when considered in terms of their components.

2. No individual is universally liked; and few individuals are completely isolated.

3. There is evidence that an individual's sociometric status is predictive of his status in the same group at a later time.

4. Sociometric status obtained in usual groups is not highly related to I.Q., M.A., C.A.; it is slightly related to skills, when these are important to the group, and to measures of social adjustment and participation.

5. Sociometric status is an index of the degree to which an individual conforms to the folkways and embodies the values of the group; it is not as close a measure of his inner psychological security.

Relationships Among Individuals in a Group

Many types of relationship can be observed from the summary sheet and show up on the target sociogram. Some of the more usual of these have been classified in the literature under the terms: isolate (2)— "outsiders" (4); leaders (2)—"stars"; reciprocated pairs—"friends" (3, 20, 21, 22); triangles, chains (6), and one-way choices—"non-friends"; two individuals with no choices from one to another—indifferents; and networks and cliques (2, 6, 7).

A consideration of specific types of relationship is a refinement from a consideration of gross scores. The question raised in studying sociometric status is broadly "Why is this person liked?" The questions raised in studying relationships are "Why is this person liked (or not liked) by this (these) other person(s)? What factors are related to this pattern and under what circumstances does this relationship flourish?" Two problems in relationships arise, one of studying characteristics of leaders, isolates, those who have friends, and those who do not, and a second of studying the inter-relationships of a leader and his followers, of friends, of an isolate and the person he chooses.

In studies of the first kind one is studying characteristics of individuals showing a certain pattern, that is characteristics of leaders (2), isolates (4), and those who have friends, or those who are "hero-worshippers." While some patterns have been studied in this way, there are considerable gaps in our knowledge. It should, for example, be quite possible to take a group of individuals who have a large proportion of their own choices reciprocated (that is, individuals who are successful in their own intimate relations) and compare them, equated on total sociometric score, with individuals whose own choices are not highly reciprocated, or to compare individuals who gave the majority of their choices to people of higher sociometric status than themselves with those who tend to choose less generally accepted persons.

From previous studies we will consider a few facts about leaders, friends, and "isolates."

Leadership patterns are built around three kinds of leaders (22): the isolated leader, the powerful leader, and the popular leader. The kind depends on what pattern of "followership" gives the leader his position (23). Leaders ("stars") resemble one another in their sensitivity and orientation to the total group but differ markedly from one another in personality (2). Some leaders show more evidence of anxiety symptoms than the average individual (17).

Friends (individuals with choices directly reciprocated) show a variety of general sociometric patterns. Among these, two have been distinguished: "X" friends, each of whom receives the bulk of his other choices from the same members of the group, and more of whose own choices are reciprocated; and "Y" friends, who receive the bulk of their choices from different people, and fewer of whose own choices are reciprocated (3).

Isolates (outsiders, underchosen). These include individuals who are chosen slightly and individuals who receive no positive choices; they may be isolated (unliked) or rejected (disliked); they may give their choices to individuals of similar status (reciprocated or unreciprocated) or give them to the stars (rarely reciprocated) (4). Some of the underchosen show personality qualities of either withdrawal from the group or aggression directed towards the group (4). They are "self-bound"; they do not contribute to the group constructively or they externalize their private discontents in hostile behaviour (2). Some of them give indications of deeper personality difficulties ranging from those psychiatrically classified as neurotic to those considered schizophrenic (24).

The second type of study consists of observing what a particular type of relationship is like; that is, how a pair of friends differ from two non-friends in the similarities and differences between the pair (3) and in the behavioural interaction they manifest in a controlled situation (25, 26, 27). For example, in comparing 21 pairs of friends with 29 pairs of similar children who were not friends, Potashin found friends and non-friends showed little difference in their similarities in height, weight, I.Q., skills; but friends talked more, jested more, and were more spontaneous.

Later studies have observed by means of a tape recorder the interaction of friends in reaching a decision, in playing without supervision, and in working on a common project, and compared this with the inter-action of non-friends in the same situation. These studies have clari-fied some of the difficulties of method.* They have also enabled us to state that in the interaction of friends there is more spontaneity, more integrative behaviour, and more evidence of relaxation and under-standing than there is in the interaction of non-friends. They also offer a tentative hypothesis, that individuals who have friends are more psychologically secure and expressive not only when they are with their friend but in other social situations (26). We suspect that the indi-vidual's capacity for forming successful intimate relationships will be a much closer index to his psychological security than with his gross sociometric status.

There is, of course, every possibility of studying other forms of rela-tionship (for example, leader-follower, isolate and the person he chooses) in terms of behavioural interaction.

In summarizing the material on sociometric relationships we may state:

1. There is a wide variety of patterns.

2. We have little evidence of which are the *best* patterns, and until we have we may assume that the one the person has developed may well be the best for him.

3. However, there is some evidence that some isolates have deeper psychological problems; that some leaders carry inner anxiety; and that individuals who have friends are apt to be generally more secure psychologically than those who have not. (19)

The Structure of the Group

The structure of the group (28) can be observed from the distribution of the scores and the actual choices among the individuals.† It is apparent from even casual inspection of distributions and sociograms that in some groups will be found many very low and very high scores whereas in other groups the scores are distributed more closely around the mean. Again, in some groups the network of choices appears to include most individuals directly or indirectly with others, in other groups choices cluster around one or two chief foci and show little other interrelation. Cleavages within groups can be measured (29, 30). A way of measuring cleavages is illustrated in the Target Sociogram

*The investigator entering on this type of study will find that certain difficulties confront him. It may save him confusion if he is warned that (1) in these studies he is matching pair with pair, not individuals with individuals and (2) it is the *interaction* of the *pair* that becomes the focus of study. He, of course, will realize that gross sociometric status becomes one of the factors which has to be equated.
†The matrix rather than the sociogram should be consulted to ascertain the basic facts.

(page 24) in which the self-preference scores for sub-groups Jews, Gentiles are calculated (28). The frequency with which different patterns (reciprocals, etc.) are found within a group should also be included in describing the group structure. Undoubtedly, sociometric facts could be used to compare structures of groups of different types—a nursery school with a camp, a classroom with another classroom, a school with an industry. It should also be possible to use sociometric structures to discover the influence of different types of group control or government. That is, the influence of controlling a group democratically or autocratically should be reflected in the group structure.

The structure of a particular situation remains remarkably *constant* (31, 32) even though the individuals in a group change in their own status, and indeed also in cases where individuals leave the group and are replaced by other individuals. For example, in studies of our nursery school continued over three years, all the children originally present have left, yet the sociograms and distributions appear remarkably similar for each of the six tests. Whether the sociometric structure reflects the social organization built by the controls of the supervisors and the programme or is the one naturally arising among nursery school children is a question which can only be answered by comparing sociograms of different types of nursery schools.

However, in studies now in progress, it has been found that groups which one would assume would be similar because the children in each one of the same age, home background, school, and grade level, show strikingly different sociometric structures. These differences are perceived by teachers as being reflected in the fact one group is "very difficult to handle" and another "very satisfactory" (see figure 5).

In order to interpret sociometric structures, a great many more investigations of structures as a whole must be made. Investigation should be undertaken soon to study the differences which appear in sociometric structures of different social groups and those which arise in the same group under different conditions. The interpretation sometimes given, that a structure is better when it shows a narrow distribution of scores, few isolates, more reciprocals and less cleavage (6), and wider networks, appears to be reasonable, but it will of course have to be checked against actual validating evidence.

With the use of the computer, matters previously insolvable are being explored. Some of the most exciting investigations are those of Dr. James Davis and his associates. They are in the process of analysing hundreds of sociograms from all over this continent and abroad by computer programming to ascertain the cohesiveness and clusterability in groups and the evolution of their structure over time.

Recent studies have considered the formal organization of a group in relation to its underlying sociometric structure. If the executives or officers who hold the formal power positions are also sociometrically chosen for those positions, the group will show high morale and function efficiently. If, however, the formal structure and sociometric structures are antagonistic, the group will deteriorate quickly or gradually. These studies have important implications for political, industrial and educational administrations which wish to develop efficient performance (30).

Conclusion

From this discussion it will be obvious that the interpretation of sociometric results is a far more complicated matter than is implied in the naive cultural assumption that "the higher the score, the better." When the various factors we have mentioned are investigated more fully, it is quite possible that sociometry will be a powerful influence in forcing us to reconsider our popular notions of social living and social values.

Already the facts lead us to discard such generalities as social adjustment, popularity, social success; to discontinue considering individuals as social or non-social; and to destroy our cultural stereotypes of the ideally socialized person. From the evidence, we must replace these with a comprehension of the infinite variety of patterns and relationships that exist, and to understand that the individual works out his social destiny in many ways.

References

1. NORTHWAY, MARY L. *What is Popularity?* Better Living Booklets. Chicago: 1955 Science Research Associates. Pp. 47.

2. JENNINGS, Helen H. *Leadership and Isolation*, 2nd edition. New York: Longmans, Green, 1950.

3. POTASHIN, REVA. "A Sociometric Study of Children's Friendships." *Sociometry*, Vol. IX (1946), No. 1, 48–70; reprinted 1947 in Sociometry Monograph No. 11.

4. NORTHWAY, MARY L. "Outsiders." *Sociometry*, Vol. VII (1944), No. 1, 429–33.

5. NORTHWAY, MARY L., and WELD, L., *Sociometric Testing: A Guide for Teachers.* Toronto: University of Toronto Press, 1957.

6. MORENO, J. L. *Who Shall Survive? A New Approach to the Problem of Human Relationships.* New York: Beacon House, 1934. Revised edition, 1953.

7. NORTHWAY, MARY L., POTASHIN, REVA, and FRANKEL, ESTHER. *Personality and Sociometric Status*, p. 56. Sociometry Monograph No. 11, 1947.

8. NORTHWAY, MARY L. "Are There Individual Differences in Social Potential?," *International Handbook of Group Psychotherapy*, Philosophical Library, New York, 1966, pp. 573–76.

9. BONNEY, M. E. "Personality Traits of Socially Successful and Unsuccessful Children." *Journal of Educational Psychology*, Vol. XXXIV (1943), No. 8, 449–72.

10. FRANKEL, ESTHER. "The Social Relationships of Pre-School Children." *Sociometry*, Vol. IX (1946), Nos. 2 and 3. Reprinted in Sociometry Monograph No. 11. See p. 24.

11. NORTHWAY, MARY L. *Appraisal of the Social Development of Children at a Summer Camp*, pp. 37f. University of Toronto Studies, Psychology Series, Vol. V (1940), No. 1.

12. BARON, D. "Personal-Social Characteristics and Classroom Social Status; A Sociometric Study of Fifth and Sixth Grade Girls." *Sociometry*, Vol. 14 (1951), No. 1, 32–42.

13. LOEB, NORA. "The Educational and Psychological Significance of Social Acceptability and its Appraisal in an Elementary School." Unpublished Ph.D. thesis, University of Toronto, 1941.

14. HILL, MARGUERITE. "A Comparative Study of the Psychometric Performance, School Achievement, Family Background, Interests and Activities of Shy and Normal Children." Unpublished M.A. thesis, University of Toronto, 1941.

15. GRAPKO, M. F. "A Study to Estimate the Degree of Relationship Between Certain Personality Traits and Social Status at a Boys' Summer Camp." Unpublished M.A. thesis, University of Toronto, 1946.

16. JOURARD, S. M. "The Relationship Between Outgoing Energy and Social Acceptance Among Children." Paper at meeting of the Canadian Psychological Association, 1949.

17. NORTHWAY, MARY L. and WIGDOR, BLOSSOM T. "Rorschach Patterns Related to the Sociometric Patterns of School Children." *Sociometry*, Vol. X (1947), No. 2, 186–99.

18. COONS, MARGERY OLSTEAD. "Rosenzweig Differences in Relation to Frustration in Children of High, Low and Middle Sociometric Status." *Group Psychotherapy*, Vol. X (March 1957), No. 1, pp. 60–63.

19. BLATZ, W. E. *Human Security: Some Reflections.* Toronto: University of Toronto Press, 1966.

20. SMITH, MAPHEUS. "Some Factors in Friendship Selection of High School Students." *Sociometry*, Vol. VII (1944), No. 3, 303–10.

21. NEUGARTEN, BERNICE. "Social class and friendship among school children." *American Journal of Sociology*, Vol. LI (1946), 305–13.

22. MORENO, J. L. "Sociometric Theory of Leadership and Isolation," in *Who Shall Survive?* Also in *Sociometry*, Vol. XIII (1950), No. 4, 382–83.

23. SEELEY, JOHN. "The Net of Reciprocal Influence" *Canadian Journal of Psychology*, Vol. 5 (1951), Nos. 1 and 2.

24. POTASHIN, REVA. "An Examination of 'Withdrawing' as a Personality Characteristic of Some Pre-adolescent Children." Unpublished Ph.D. thesis, University of Toronto, 1951.

25. CAMPBELL, ELEANOR M. "A Study of Differences in Interaction Patterns of Pairs of Children Chosen According to Sociometric Relationships." Unpublished M.A. thesis, University of Toronto, 1951.

26. GRAHAM, JOYCE P. "A study of laughter as a form of interaction between children of defined sociometric relationships." Unpublished M.A. thesis, University of Toronto, 1951.

27. MILLER, CHARLOTTE H. "A Study of Social Interaction of Pre-school Children Paired According to Sociometric Ratings." Unpublished M.A. thesis, University of Toronto, 1951.

28. CRISWELL, JOAN. "The Measurement of Group Intergration." *Sociometry*, Vol. X (1947), 259–67. Reprinted in the *Sociometry Reader*, pp. 252–60.

29. —— "A Sociometric Study of Race Cleavage in the Classroom." *Archives of Psychology*, Vol. 33 (1939), No. 235.

30. JENNINGS, HELEN H. "Sociometric Choice Process in Personality and Group Formation" in the *Sociometry Reader*. Glencoe: Free Press, pp. 87–112.

31. QUARRINGTON, M. O., "Developmental Aspects of Sociometric Ratings of Nursery School Children." Unpublished M.A. thesis, University of Toronto, 1953.

32. THOMSON, MARY. "An analysis of the sociometric ratings of groups of children from three to eight years of age." M.A. thesis, University of Toronto, 1948. (Published in abstract in *Twenty-Five Years of Child Study*, University of Toronto Press, 1951, p. 173.)

See also the section on "Community, Industry, and the Armed Forces," edited by C. P. Loomis and C. H. Procter, in *The Sociometry Reader*, pp. 471–567, for descriptions of structures of various types of graphs; also K. M. Evans, chapter 5 on "Leadership," in *Sociometry and Education*, for her insightful distinction between leadership and headship.

9
What does sociometry measure?

THE FIRST EIGHT SECTIONS of this book have been based on facts from the story of sociometry as it has evolved in the last thirty years. The reader has the clues by which he can solve the mystery of what sociometry measures and what sociometric discoveries mean. That at this point he may be unable to do so is largely the result of a "red herring" which was drawn into sociometry early in its development and for which we are at least partly responsible. The establishment of total scores and the development of our thinking around these has been in some ways a distraction which has led us farther and farther away from fundamental sociometric facts. That scoring methods were and are essential no one can doubt. They "brought order out of chaos" and enabled the data to be organized in manageable ways. They promoted much valuable research and provided an incentive for developing statistical methods capable of handling the complexity of social data. But the assumption that an individual's sociometric score, whether calculated by the crudest or by the most refined techniques, is a measure of his acceptance *by the group*, is, if not a fallacy, at least a not wholly true interpretation of sociometric facts.

Actually, a sociometric score is not a measure of the degree to which an individual is accepted by *a group*. The group has never been asked to reach a common decision as to whom it, as a group, most preferred. The group has never expressed an opinion regarding its rating of its individual members. A sociometric score is in essence *the number of times an individual has been chosen by other individuals as a preferred associate for certain actions*. The only facts of sociometry are the choices made by individuals to other individuals. If we are clear in our understanding of this we begin to gain insight into what sociometry is measuring. Our basic question is no longer why is A accepted to the *x* degree by the group, but rather why is A chosen by B, C, D, and K. If we could discover for what qualities A was chosen by B, C, D, and K and not chosen by Q, R, S, and T, we would commence the discovery of what sociometry is measuring.*

To begin our search for an answer let us reduce the problem to the

*Moreno himself stated this in his original work and despite his appreciation of statistical advances, he has maintained consistently that sociometry is measuring the inter-relationships among individuals; the attractions and repulsions or in his terms the "tele" effect. The sociometric essence of a group is the tele effect among the individuals.

simplest facts: on a given test it is discovered that A chooses B and therefore B is chosen by A. The only act that has occurred is that A chooses B. Most of our previous effort has been to understand why B is chosen; it would appear profitable to reverse this question and focus our interest on the chooser by asking why does A choose B?

Obviously A makes a choice because we have presented him with a stimulus situation that provokes one. He may never have considered with whom he most wished to work before; he certainly may not have expressed it. It may startle some modern social scientists to realize that in presenting this choice situation we are doing nothing essentially different from what was done in the traditional psychological laboratory procedures, initiated long ago by Weber, Fechner, and Wundt, when the subject was asked to discriminate between two lights, colours, sounds, etc., and to choose one. To answer the question "With whom of these people do you choose to associate?" involves exactly the same *psychological process* as to state which of two sounds is the higher. It assumes the subject can discriminate or has the ability to choose. Therefore to answer the question "Why does A choose B?" takes us into a consideration of the nature of *the psychology of choice* and its relation to sociometry.

One of the facts of modern psychology is that human experiencing is in its essence selective. Unable to assimilate the total environment the organism absorbs those aspects of it which are most appropriate to it; those which satisfy its needs and enhance its organization. This point of view is implied by many of the dynamic psychologists; it is proclaimed as fundamental and elucidated in detail by Sir Frederick Bartlett whose book *Remembering* (1) is less well known on this continent than it might profitably be.

Bartlett considers selectivity to be the basic characteristic of psychological life. The individual through his perceptual processes selects items of his environment and modifies them in such a fashion that they fit the pattern of his dynamic experience. It is not the object *per se* that determines whether it will be selected or not, but rather the individual pattern as it is functioning at that time, with the particular needs, attitudes, emotions, purposes, and aspirations that are dominating. Such patterns are conscious, although they are influenced by unconscious processes such as physiological and neurological conditions, and they contain a time dimension which means that they include remembrance of things past and anticipation of things to come.

A recent discussion of Bartlett's theory, its relation to the psychoanalytic point of view and to the concept of cognitive style is discussed by I. H. Irving (2). It has also been pointed out locally that social selectivity is compatible with Blatz's security theory (3), in which decision making (one form of which is choosing comparisons) followed by its consequence, is the basis of learning; and the willingness to accept the consequence is the essence of mental health. The consequence of a sociometric choice is the chosen person's reaction. Thus the consequences become circular, or perhaps it is better to call them spiral. The acceptance of interweaving consequences of such choices among individuals may well be considered fundamental in social health. It has also been suggested by Schermann that current studies of young children's discrimination (4) might well be related to their "discrimination' or preference for companions; that ability to discriminate cognitive objects and to select social objects may follow similar developmental patterns. This thought introduces a number of intriguing speculations and gives rise to some novel hypotheses which might be investigated fruitfully.

To expand these points of view further would lead into a discussion of psychological theory which is inappropriate here. For our purposes it is sufficient to show that this idea of selectivity is important because it makes sense out of sociometry. The individual, being selective by nature, selects social objects in the same manner he selects from the non-social environment and he transforms these perceptually so they satisfy or enhance his experience. The reason for the selection is not in the selected but in the selector. Social value, like beauty, is in the eyes of the beholder. This statement was tested by Detweiler in a study of children's perception of friends and those who are not their friends. She shows that children perceive those they choose sociometrically to rate higher on such traits as honesty, generosity and good sportsmanship than those to whom they are indifferent (5).

Sociometry is therefore primarily measuring or at least discovering, what needs an individual has for personal social companionship; whereas sociometric scores as traditionally used are a projection of measurement from the subject to the object, an attempt to rate social value rather than social want.

A shift of emphasis from the chosen to the chooser clarifies some very interesting facts of sociometry. Anyone who is familiar with sociometric testing is aware that in any test there is often one individual who is ignored by most of the group and who appears even to the tester to be a most "unattractive," dull, stupid, clumsy, uninteresting and tedious person, yet he does receive one choice. Why? Certainly not because of his possession of the culture's fictitious social values; rather because in the experience of the chooser he is seen as satisfying some need or enhancing some activity. It is true the chooser's need in such a case may be to express kindness, to be able to feel sorry for, to dominate, or to possess a liege-man. That clinical psychology has led us to be suspicious of such motives makes not one iota of difference to the fact that they establish genuine social bonds. Indeed anyone who fulfils a need

or enriches the experience of another individual on any basis whatso-
ever possesses social value and forms a part of the structure that
becomes in its totality the great society.

Sociometry, in the discovery of social need and its fulfilment, will
clarify our understanding of social facts far more than sociometric
scores ever have done. Sociometric scores, evaluating a person in terms
of the frequency he is chosen, are all too easily interpreted according
to the folklore of our culture, which identifies goodness with power and
greatness with prestige. Sociometry, in turning to study the chooser,
discovers that humans differ in their needs for social experience as they
differ in all other aspects of their experience; it understands that A
chooses B because A having needs, wants, desires, and purposes, and
having the ability to discriminate, interprets B as the object which gives
him most satisfaction and perceives qualities in B which are valuable
to himself.

As Jennings (6) has so ably described in her discussion of the
psychogroup and sociogroup, individuals choose different persons to
meet different needs; thus the persons they prefer to associate with in
a work situation may be quite different from those whom they would
like for intimate companions.

The series of studies summarized by Taguiri on individuals accuracy
in perceiving the extent to which they were accepted, ignored, or
rejected should also be mentioned (7). Sociometry measures primarily
who chooses whom; "perceptual sociometry" examines how individuals
consider themselves to be chosen, the similarities and discrepancies
between the way an individual is liked or disliked and how he thinks
he is liked or disliked has opened a wide field of research and enhanced
the whole concept of empathy.

If sociometry is to progress further, its study must be of the inter-
relationships between individuals, all types and conditions of them. In
non-social situations the individual is selecting from a non-responsive
environment, but in sociometry each object under scrutiny has its own
property of selectivity: A as an individual selecting colour, food, or
poetry from his environment makes his choice and fits it into his
experience; A as an individual selecting B from his social environment
is entangled with the fact that B is also selective, and may select,
ignore, or reject him. The fundamental difference between social
psychology and individual psychology is the potential selectivity of all
the objects involved. Reciprocal relationships (or the social selection
by two objects of one another) is found nowhere else. This indicates
the need for studying choices in terms not only of the person who
makes them, but of the responses he obtains from the chosen. It is
possible that reciprocal relations expressed in marriage, friendship,
working associations, or around avocational interests are, from the

pre-school years on, the most satisfying of all human achievements. For the experiences of each individual are continually enhanced by the responsive actions of others. The basic bond of society may consist in the fact that individuals like each other. However, this fully reciprocated relationship is only one specialized form among the countless variations found in sociometric patterns. What these are, how they function, and the ways by which the needs of different individuals are satisfied through the various forms offer an intriguing area of study for future development.

What then does sociometry measure? In its basic procedure sociometry does not measure, it *discovers.* It is essentially a technique for locating the relationships which are formed between individuals. Sociometric scores, of course, do measure; they measure the number of relationships of which an individual is part, but not the intensity of these. They therefore measure the width but not the depth of his social value; in other words, they measure the extent to which he is perceived by others as fulfilling their needs, or enhancing their experience.

References

1. BARTLETT, F. C. *Remembering: A Study of Social and Experimental Psychology.* Cambridge, 1932.
2. IRVING, I. H. "Studies in Remembering." *Psychological Issues*, Vol. I, No. 2, 1959.
3. BLATZ, W. E. *Human Security: Some Reflections.* University of Toronto Press, Toronto, 1966.
4. SCHERMANN, ADA. "Discrimination in Young Children." *Child Study* (The Bulletin of the Institute of Child Study), Vol. XXIX, No. 2, 1967, pp. 2–11.
5. NORTHWAY, MARY L. and DETWEITER, JOYCE. "Children's Perception of Friends and Non-Friends," *Sociometry and the Science of Man.* Beacon House, 1956, pp. 27–31.
6. JENNINGS, HELEN H. *Leadership and Isolation,* 2nd edition. New York, Longmans, 1950.
7. TAGUIRI, R. "Perceptual Sociometry." *The Sociometry Reader.* Glencoe Free Press, pp. 568–704.

10
The contribution of sociometry

MANY SOCIAL SCIENTISTS, contrary to some of their declarations, are idealists and moralists; they are hopeful that the facts they discover will be immediately or remotely useful in establishing a better society than that of the present and enabling man to live with a greater degree of satisfaction. Sociometry can, in a number of ways, contribute to our understanding of social living and thus to the achievement of these wider aims.

First there is the fact of *preference.* Human beings do not and cannot love each other equally. From early childhood the individual prefers a few people of the many that make up the world. To others he is indifferent, antagonistic, and indeed of the great majority ignorant. This being a fact, it is important to accept preferences, whether they fit into our preconceived idea of what society should be or not. We must no longer pretend that a child must be a friend to everyone, nor that the adult must feel a *personal* concern for every other human being. He cannot; and if he tries to do so, he develops a superficial pseudo-socialization which has little meaning or, when he fails, is nagged by a remorseful sense of guilt.

If preferences are inevitable it is important that we accept them; if we are to develop a good society, however, it is also important that we neither confuse them with prejudice nor substitute them for justice.

If it is true that out of any group an individual prefers a few with whom to establish personal relationships, he will have to learn to be as just to those he does not prefer as to those he does. He will have to learn when he is very young to let another child have the toy, not because he likes him and wishes to bestow it, but because it is the other child's right and his turn. Later he will have to learn to work on a project as fairly with those who are not his preferred companions as with those who are. Gradually a concern for people because of their common humanity and not because of their sociometric desirability to him will have to grow. To be considerate, kind, generous, and loyal, to those to whom we are sociometrically attached is relatively simple. To strive for justice, to seek the welfare of those to whom we are sociometrically indifferent is to attempt to follow the more difficult of the Great Commandments. How the aims of justice and human welfare are to be accomplished and include the fact of human preference is a salient problem for social research.

Nor does the fact of preference imply that individuals in any particular situation are being prejudiced. Prejudice is a prejudgment which places an artificial limitation on preferences and rationalizes this limitation on the basis of some culturally held value. A person may choose as an associate anyone he knows. A child may wish to play with anyone on the street. If we say to him you mustn't play with Jimmy (because he is not of the right class), or Solly (because he is a Jew), or Peter (because his father gets drunk), and he accepts our instruction, we have attempted to set a limit to the areas in which preference may extend.

On the other hand, one should be extremely careful in interpreting preferences as prejudices. If a white child does not choose a Negro, this may be because of a prejudice against Negroes, or it may be because he has no preference for any particular Negro. It should be remembered that among white children there are also many he does not choose. Studies of preference may possibly be essential in order to understand and to deal wisely with prejudice. Indeed, in all our studies of sub-groups in classrooms we have found that, in spite of the predominantly self-preference scores of these groups, some preferences are made across cleavage lines. These bonds may be the foundations for inter-group understanding and co-operation.

Yet, in this era of the 1960s, when violence has erupted in the North American continent in race riots, senseless murders, tragic assassinations and the like, has sociometry not more to say than it has to this point? In its concentration on well-defined groups, the classroom particularly, and on others in which sophisticated statistics may be neatly applied, has it neglected its potential contribution to the understanding of groups precipitated into violent action? Has the sociometric structure of present-day society changed? Do current intrepersonal relations reflect those described in the text books? Now that its techniques have become polished and its mathematics respectable, would it not be profitable for sociometry to investigate the structure of the huge apartment block, the sprawling vast industry, the suburban neighbourhood, the ghettos, the separatists, and indeed the Eskimos and Indians of Canada and the negro-white relationships of the United States? As social chaos has increased, have sociometric relationships broken down? What, for instance, would a sociogram of the hippies look like? These matters of social significance and understanding appear to be the great concern to which the next generation of sociometrists might well direct their efforts. "What's past is prologue." Technical means have been refined in the last forty years. The technique is now ready to be used to gain insight into a society which is creating havoc from its own efforts while living under the dual threats of extermination by a nuclear bomb from without and of deterioration by the pollution of its interpersonal relations from within.

Preference for association is natural to human beings and gives rise to their great creative efforts. But without justice in human affairs, preferences may become ends in themselves and finally dissipate in a surfeit of turbulence. Humanity will then no longer be made up of social beings, but will regress to a mass of self-striving individuals motivated by their hostilities to one another.

A *second* contribution of sociometry is that it implicitly assumes that the individual is, or becomes, *conscious* of his preferences. Even at two years of age the child consciously states that he wants to play with Johnny. It is true that he may not be aware of the reasons for his choice. Indeed, if he is asked he may state only "because he is nice" or "because I like him." However, whether or not he knows his motives, he does know his preference. Possibly even as adults the reasons we attach to our preferences are merely attempts to justify a relationship in terms of cultural values. For the adult erroneously believes preferences need justification. Actually they never need to be explained, only accepted. And in the final analysis the cause of social selectivity will probably remain one of the most difficult questions to answer; the essence of affiliations is as difficult to fully explain scientifically as is the essential nature of growth or the meaning of life itself.

Nevertheless, the preference itself is conscious. In basing its approach on this premise, sociometry develops a theory of human meaning which is directly opposite to that of psychoanalysis. This theory assumes that his consciously known living relationships are of major importance to the individual, and that the earlier relationship to his mother in infancy or to his father at his oedipus stage has historical rather than dynamic meaning.

Sociometry considers all relationships as means by which the individual extends himself, and society a means by which he can satisfy his needs and enhance his experience. The early psychoanalytic doctrine which considers society an oppressing and stultifying prison is replaced by a view of society as a potentially rich soil out of which the individual derives nutriment for his growth and the sustenance necessary for an enriched life. His conscious relationships are his attempts to ask, to seek, and to find a life which is both richer than himself and through which he himself grows greater.

One more fact is basic in sociometry. Sociometry assumes that social relationships have a time dimension. The questions asked on most tests imply this. "With whom would you like to cabin?" considers not only the moment but the camp period; "With whom would you like to work?" not only this morning but for to-morrow and to-morrow. While actual preferences, as has been demonstrated in the studies, wax and wane, they show a remarkable durability. As man is the organism that seriously contemplates the future, as his actions are controlled to a greater extent by his purposes than by his "conditioning," he includes in his preferences a sense of anticipation. His selections are made not only in terms of how his chosen associate serves him *now* but in terms of what he may help him to be. As what he is to become is to himself, if not to the scientists or clinician, always more important than what he has been, and as where he is going is more significant than whence he has come, he has in his relationships a means by which he may more fully *be* himself and more rightly *reach* his destiny. From this fact there is hope that human society will not be vanquished or destroy itself. The inter-relatedness of human beings may be the rock foundation which endures despite the increasing maelstroms of social chaos.

So at the end we reach the prime fact of sociometry—the answer to the question, "Who Shall Survive?" John Donne forecast this answer over three hundred years ago in his *Devotions*: "No man is an Iland, intire of itselfe; every man is a peece of the Continent, a part of the maine . . . I am involved in all Mankinde." Sociometry simply demonstrates that the fundamental bonds which hold man to the Continent are his own personal relationships. Such bonds do not grow from society's attempt to chain him, but out of his own need to free himself from his own insularity in a security which is greater than himself and through which he himself becomes greater. In this end, perhaps, lies the beginning.

Appendix A

Suggested problems for research

The Test Itself

(a) *Administration and construction*

1. The effect on the sociometric scores obtained of varying the number of criteria and/or the number of choices required.
2. The effect of different types of criteria—general, particular, etc.
3. The comparative effects of administering the test individually and in a group.
4. The influence of preliminary instructions.
5. The influence of using prepared test forms compared with merely reading each question aloud to the subjects.
6. The effect of repeating the same test compared with using alternative forms.
7. The effect of immediate use of the results in the practical setting.
8. The effect of using "negative choices"; ways and means for introducing these to minimize resentment.
9. The effect of the administrator.

(b) *Scoring*

1. A comparison of "weighted" and "unweighted" scores.
2. Weighting in terms of the social power of the chooser.
3. Weighting in terms of intensity of the choice.

(c) *Reliability and validity*

1. Study of the intercorrelations between test items.
2. Study of use of alternative forms of the test.
3. Studies of repetition of the test; influence of time intervals.
4. Studies of results on the test compared with choices made in actual situations.

(d) *Distributions*

1. Studies of distribution of scores; comparisons of same group at different times; comparison of different groups.
2. Influence of combining negative and/or positive choices.
3. Influence of increasing number of choices to a total approximating the number of individuals in the group.

Theoretical Studies

(a) *Sociometric status*

1. Analysis of the component patterns underlying similar gross scores.
2. Relation of scores to various outside criteria: (1) behaviour; (2) adult judgments; (3) objective factors; (4) measures of social adjustment; (5) measures of psychological security.
3. A comparison of an individual's sociometric status in different groups among which there is a minimum of overlap.
4. A comparison of an individual's sociometric status at different age levels—pre-school to adult level.

(b) *Sociometric relationships*

1. Studies of characteristics—objective, behavioural, social, psychological —as they appear in individuals having certain types of relationships.
2. Studies of the correspondence in characteristics of the two or more individuals forming a particular type of relationship.
3. Studies of interaction between individuals forming a particular type of relationship.
4. Descriptions of a person given by individuals who choose him in different relationships. Comparison with descriptions by people who do not choose him.
5. Length of endurance of reciprocated relationships, compared with non-reciprocated. Length of endurance at different age levels.
6. Studies of entire "social atoms."

(c) *Group structures*

1. The constancy of the group structure within a given organization.
2. A comparison of sociometric structures *(a)* in different groups and organizations (camps, schools, industries, etc.) in our own culture; *(b)* in our own and other cultures; and *(c)* at different age levels.
3. The effect on group structure of different kinds of administration, e.g. democratic, autocratic.
4. The study of cleavage into sub-groups on the basis of sex, ethnic background, religion, etc.
5. The sociometry of small groups.
6. The changes in group structure occurring with the addition or removal of a "key" individual from the group.

Practical Studies

1. The effect of arranging groups on basis of sociometric preference. Measures of behaviour and security resulting.
2. Ways and means of "helping" the "isolate" and the "leader."
3. Use of the person chosen in aiding socialization.
4. How to set up "therapeutic" groups, reports of their activities, and evaluation of results.

Appendix B

Suggestions for reporting a sociometric study

BEFORE using sociometry in a research study, it is strongly advised that the investigator should have some previous practice with it. As a minimum requirement he should construct, administer, score, and interpret at least one test; preferably a great many more.

A report of any sociometric study should include the following facts:

1. A description of the group; number of subjects; age range, sex; type of organization; length of time group has been together.
2. The exact criteria used and number of choices allowed. (Note number of choices if any omitted.)
3. The exact instructions given and the form of administration, and by whom it was administered.
4. The number of absentees at time of the test; what was done about them.
5. Questions raised by the group or difficulties encountered in giving the test.
6. How the test was scored.
7. The matrix of the scores.
8. A distribution of the scores.
9. The intercorrelations obtained on the items.
10. Other measures used to estimate reliability.
11. Any measures of validity used.
12. The frequency of common types of relationship; isolate; reciprocate pairs: one way choices, etc.
13. A sociogram of the group.

Obviously all these details will not be expected in a final published account of the study. They should, however, be included by students and, indeed, by more advanced investigators, in the typed or mimeographed reports on which publications will be based.

Appendix C

Additional notes

A note on statistics

As THIS IS a *primer* the aims of brevity and clarity have in places led to over-simplification, particularly in the sections on statistics. The research worker is strongly advised to consider the phenomenon of the skewed distribution more fully, in terms both of the statistical factors which cause and of the other factors which accentuate its positive skewness. It should be pointed out also that the constant frame of reference which we have used as the basis of our discussion is a matter of controversy among sociometrists. The reader should consult Criswell, Joan, "Notes on the Constant Frame of Reference Problem," *Sociometry*, Vol. XIII (1950), No. 2, 93–107, and "Sociometric Concepts in Personnel Administration," *ibid.*, Vol. XII (1949), No. 4, 287–300.

The section on Method in *The Sociometry Reader* (pp. 133–400) will prove an excellent entry to problems of measurement and provides many references to original sources. For those interested in more advanced mathematics, recent numbers of the *Sociometry Journal*, as well as *Mathematical Methods in Small Group Processes* (edited by Joan Criswell, Herbert Solomon, and Patrick S. Chanford, University Press, 1962, pp. viii and 361, should be consulted.

A note on applications of sociometry

Since this Primer was first written much has appeared on applying sociometric findings in human situations. As would be expected, a majority of these reports are descriptive of the use of sociometric information in schools and similar settings. However, they have not been limited to these. It is to be hoped that a journal of applied sociometry may be published one day that will channel the findings from the many sources of applied areas through one outlet. The reader who is interested in applications might well begin by consulting Helen Jennings, *Sociometry in Group Relations* (2nd edition, American Council on Education, Washington, D.C., 1959) and K. M. Evans (*Sociometry and Education*, Routledge and Kegan Paul, 1962) and by following the reference contained in these volumes.
